EVERYMAN, I will go with thee, and be thy guide,
In thy most need to go by thy side

EVERYMAN CLASSICS

EDWARD LEAR,
LEWIS CARROLL AND OTHERS

A Book of Nonsense

Edited by Ernest Rhys

Introduction by
Roger Lancelyn Green

J. M. Dent Sons Ltd: London
EVERYMAN'S LIBRARY

Made in Great Britain by
Guernsey Press Co. Ltd., Guernsey, C.I. for
J. M. Dent & Sons Ltd
91 Clapham High Street, London SW4 7TA

This volume was first published in
Everyman's Library in 1927
Last reprinted 1988

No 806 Hardback ISBN 0 460 00806 4
No 1806 Paperback ISBN 0 460 11806 4

INTRODUCTION

As one might expect in a book of nonsense, the earliest item in this collection is one of the latest. Edward Lear (1812–88) began his career as a serious artist by making minutely accurate paintings of the Parrots in Lord Derby's collection at Knowsley; but when he grew tired of this serious occupation, he amused the children of the house by writing limericks for them and drawing quick, humorous illustrations to suit each of the quaint characters and situations which he described. *A Book of Nonsense* was first published in 1846 and the revised and enlarged edition used here appeared in 1863.

By this time Lewis Carroll (1832–98), who was really that serious mathematical student the Rev. Charles Lutwidge Dodgson, had written *Alice's Adventures in Wonderland* (it was published in 1865). Most of the nonsense verses in it were parodies of the serious poems and songs which the three little girls for whom he wrote the story knew quite well. It is amusing to find in their new dress "How doth the little busy bee" and "'Tis the voice of the sluggard" by Isaac Watts (1715), "You are old, Father William," by Robert Southey (1799), Jane Taylor's "Twinkle, twinkle little star" (1806), Mary Hewitt's "Will you walk into my parlour said the Spider to the Fly" (1834), "Speak gently to the little child" (*c.* 1848) by David Bates, and "Beautiful Star," the popular song by J. M. Sayles. "They told me you had been to her" was written by Lewis Carroll many years earlier, and published in 1855; but he is not the author of "The Queen of Hearts," which was an old nursery rhyme, first printed (with three other verses) in *The European Magazine* in April 1782.

The *Nonsense Rhymes* in Part VIII are also mostly very old, and their authors are quite unknown. Many of them were included in *Mother Goose's Melody* (1765) but the fullest collection was made by James Orchard Halliwell who published *The Nursery Rhymes of England* in 1842, and followed it by bigger and better collections until 1860. From this comes the prose tale "Lazy Jack," and most of the verses in the section called *The Jolly Beggar*—though the beggar himself (who was originally "Jovial") comes from an old song, as does "Lavender's Blue," which was first printed about 1680. "The Cheat of Cupid," on the other hand, is by the poet Robert Herrick (1591–1674) and was included in his *Hesperides* (1648). Some of the other verses are also the works of well-known poets: "Pigwiggen" is a short section from Michael Drayton's fairy poem *Nymphidia* (1627), "Robin Goodfellow" was published anonymously about 1600, and was thought to be by Ben Jonson; "Farewell to the Fairies" was by Bishop Robert Corbet (1648), " An Elegy on the Death of a Mad Dog" comes from Goldsmith's *The Vicar of Wakefield* (1766), while "The Old Man of the Sea" and "The Ballad of the Oysterman" are by the American poet Oliver Wendell Holmes (1809–94). "Bobby Bingo" is a traditional song of unknown date and authorship.

Struwwelpeter first appeared in English in 1848, three years after the German original by Dr. Heinrich Hoffman, but who translated it is unknown. The dramatist Samuel Foote (1720–1777) had already written "The Great Panjandrum," and another German, Rudolf Erich Raspe (1737–94), told (in English) of *The Adventures of Baron Munchausen* (1785).

"The Strange Journey of Tuflongbo" comes from the seventh chapter of *Legends from Fairyland* by "Holme Lee" (Harriet Parr, 1828–1900), published in 1860. The version here printed has been shortened and altered—making it more amusing and nonsensical than the original.

Our collection is completed by a selection from the *Lilliput Levee* (1864) of William Brighty Rands, and the *Nursery Nonsense, or Rhymes without Reason* (1864), by the classical scholar D'Arcy Wentworth Thompson.

"You may call it 'nonsense' if you like," said the Red Queen, "but *I've* heard nonsense compared with which that would be as sensible as a dictionary!"

ROGER LANCELYN GREEN.

CONTENTS

A BOOK OF NONSENSE

BY

EDWARD LEAR

TO THE

GREAT-GRANDCHILDREN, GRAND-NEPHEWS,
AND GRAND-NIECES OF EDWARD,
13th EARL OF DERBY,

THIS BOOK OF DRAWINGS AND VERSES

(The greater part of which were originally made
and composed for their parents)

IS DEDICATED BY THE AUTHOR,

EDWARD LEAR.

LONDON,

1863.

There was an Old Man with a beard,
Who said, "It is just as I feared!—
Two Owls and a Hen,
Four Larks and a Wren,
Have all built their nests in my beard!"

There was a Young Lady of Ryde,
Whose shoe-strings were seldom untied:
She purchased some clogs,
And some small spotty dogs,
And frequently walked about Ryde.

There was an Old Man with a nose,
Who said, "If you choose to suppose,
  That my nose is too long,
  You are certainly wrong!"
That remarkable Man with a nose.

There was an Old Man on a hill,
Who seldom, if ever, stood still;
  He ran up and down,
  In his Grandmother's gown,
Which adorned that Old Man on a hill.

There was a Young Lady whose bonnet
Came untied when the birds sate upon it;
But she said, "I don't care!
All the birds in the air
Are welcome to sit on my bonnet!"

There was a Young Person of Smyrna,
Whose Grandmother threatened to burn her;
But she seized on the Cat,
And said, "Granny, burn that!
You incongruous Old Woman of Smyrna!"

There was an Old Person of Chili,
Whose conduct was painful and silly,
He sate on the stairs,
Eating apples and pears,
That imprudent Old Person of Chili.

There was an Old Man with a gong,
Who bumped at it all the day long;
But they called out, "O law!
You're a horrid old bore!"
So they smashed that Old Man with a gong.

There was an Old Lady of Chertsey,
Who made a remarkable curtsey;
  She twirled round and round,
  Till she sunk underground,
Which distressed all the people of Chertsey.

There was an Old Man in a tree,
Who was horribly bored by a Bee;
  When they said, "Does it buzz?"
  He replied, "Yes, it does!
It's a regular brute of a Bee!"

There was an Old Man with a flute,
A sarpint ran into his boot;
  But he played day and night,
  Till the sarpint took flight,
And avoided that Man with a flute.

There was a Young Lady whose chin
Resembled the point of a pin:
  So she had it made sharp,
  And purchased a harp,
And played several tunes with her chin.

There was an Old Man of Kilkenny,
Who never had more than a penny;
He spent all that money
In onions and honey,
That wayward Old Man of Kilkenny.

There was an Old Person of Ischia,
Whose conduct grew friskier and friskier;
He danced hornpipes and jigs,
And ate thousands of figs,
That lively Old Person of Ischia.

There was an Old Man in a boat,
Who said, "I'm afloat! I'm afloat!"
When they said, "No! you ain't!"
He was ready to faint,
That unhappy Old Man in a boat.

There was a Young Lady of Portugal,
Whose ideas were excessively nautical:
She climbed up a tree,
To examine the sea,
But declared she would never leave Portugal.

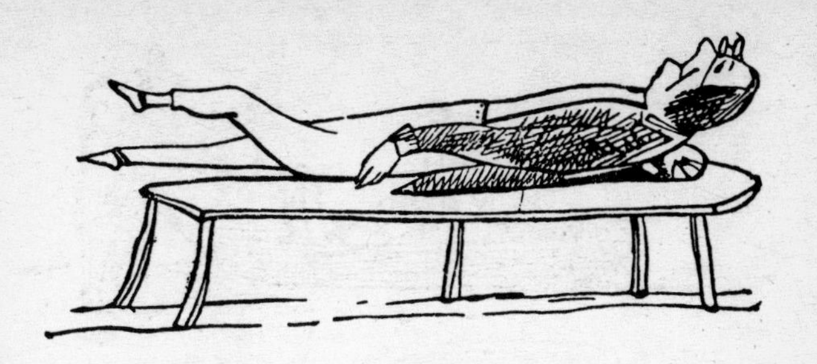

There was an Old Man of Moldavia,
Who had the most curious behaviour;
For while he was able,
He slept on a table,
That funny Old Man of Moldavia.

There was an Old Man of Madras,
Who rode on a cream-coloured ass;
But the length of its ears
So promoted his fears,
That it killed that Old Man of Madras.

There was an Old Person of Leeds,
Whose head was infested with beads;
She sat on a stool,
And ate gooseberry fool,
Which agreed with that Person of Leeds.

There was an Old Man of Peru,
Who never knew what he should do;
So he tore off his hair,
And behaved like a bear,
That intrinsic Old Man of Peru.

There was an Old Person of Hurst,
Who drank when he was not athirst;
When they said, "You'll grow fatter,"
He answered, "What matter?"
That globular Person of Hurst.

There was a Young Person of Crete,
Whose toilette was far from complete;
She dressed in a sack,
Spickle-speckled with black,
That ombliferous Person of Crete.

There was an Old Man of the Isles,
Whose face was pervaded with smiles:
He sung high dum diddle,
And played on the fiddle,
That amiable Man of the Isles.

There was an Old Person of Buda,
Whose conduct grew ruder and ruder;
Till at last, with a hammer,
They silenced his clamour,
By smashing that Person of Buda.

There was an Old Man of Columbia,
Who was thirsty, and called out for some beer;
But they brought it quite hot,
In a small copper pot,
Which disgusted that Man of Columbia.

There was a Young Lady of Dorking,
Who bought a large bonnet for walking;
But its colour and size
So bedazzled her eyes,
That she very soon went back to Dorking.

There was an Old Man who supposed,
That the street door was partially closed;
But some very large rats
Ate his coats and his hats,
While that futile old gentleman dozed.

There was an Old Man of the West,
Who wore a pale plum-coloured vest;
When they said, "Does it fit?"
He replied, "Not a bit!"
That uneasy Old Man of the West.

There was an Old Man of the Wrekin,
Whose shoes made a horrible creaking;
But they said, "Tell us, whether,
Your shoes are of leather,
Or of what, you Old Man of the Wrekin?"

There was a Young Lady whose eyes
Were unique as to colour and size;
When she opened them wide,
People all turned aside,
And started away in surprise.

There was a Young Lady of Norway,
Who casually sat in a doorway;
When the door squeezed her flat,
She exclaimed, "What of that?"
This courageous Young Lady of Norway

There was an Old Man of Vienna,
Who lived upon Tincture of Senna;
When that did not agree,
He took Camomile Tea,
That nasty Old Man of Vienna.

There was an Old Person whose habits
Induced him to feed upon Rabbits;
When he'd eaten eighteen,
He turned perfectly green,
Upon which he relinquished those habits.

There was an Old Person of Dover,
Who rushed through a field of blue Clover:
But some very large bees
Stung his nose and his knees,
So he very soon went back to Dover.

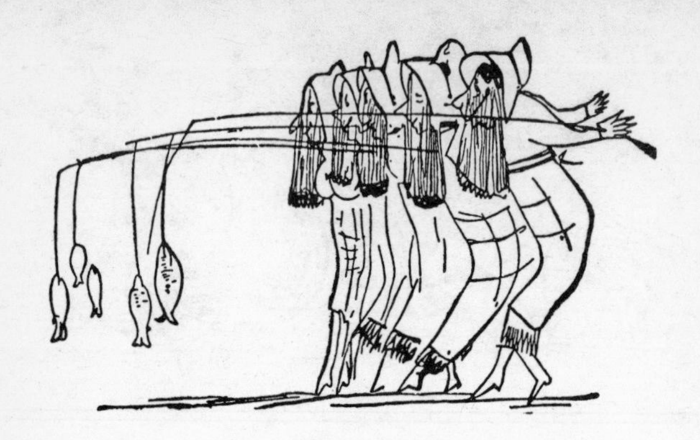

There was an Old Man of Marseilles,
Whose daughters wore bottle-green veils;
They caught several Fish,
Which they put in a dish,
And sent to their Pa' at Marseilles.

There was an Old Person of Cadiz,
Who was always polite to all ladies;
But in handing his daughter,
He fell into the water,
Which drowned that Old Person of Cadiz.

There was an Old Person of Basing,
Whose presence of mind was amazing;
He purchased a steed,
Which he rode at full speed,
And escaped from the people of Basing.

There was an Old Man of Quebec,
A beetle ran over his neck;
But he cried, "With a needle,
I'll slay you, O beadle!"
That angry Old Man of Quebec.

There was an Old Person of Philœ,
Whose conduct was scroobious and wily;
He rushed up a Palm,
When the weather was calm,
And observed all the ruins of Philœ.

There was a Young Lady of Bute,
Who played on a silver-gilt flute;
She played several jigs
To her uncle's white pigs,
That amusing Young Lady of Bute.

There was a Young Lady whose nose
Was so long that it reached to her toes:
So she hired an Old Lady,
Whose conduct was steady,
To carry that wonderful nose.

There was a Young Lady of Turkey,
Who wept when the weather was murky;
When the day turned out fine,
She ceased to repine,
That capricious Young Lady of Turkey.

There was an Old Man of Apulia,
Whose conduct was very peculiar;
He fed twenty sons
Upon nothing but buns,
That whimsical Man of Apulia.

There was an Old Man with a poker,
Who painted his face with red oker;
When they said, "You're a Guy!"
He made no reply,
But knocked them all down with his poker.

There was an Old Person of Prague,
Who was suddenly seized with the plague;
    But they gave him some butter,
    Which caused him to mutter,
And cured that Old Person of Prague.

There was an Old Man of the North,
Who fell into a basin of broth;
    But a laudable cook
    Fished him out with a hook,
Which saved that Old Man of the North.

There was a Young Lady of Poole,
Whose soup was excessively cool;
So she put it to boil,
By the aid of some oil,
That ingenious Young Lady of Poole.

There was an Old Person of Mold,
Who shrank from sensations of cold;
So he purchased some muffs,
Some furs and some fluffs,
And wrapped himself from the cold.

There was an Old Man of Nepaul,
From his horse had a terrible fall;
  But, though split quite in two,
  By some very strong glue,
They mended that Man of Nepaul.

There was an Old Man of th' Abruzzi,
So blind that he couldn't his foot see;
  When they said, "That's your toe,"
  He replied, "Is it so?"
That doubtful Old Man of th' Abruzzi.

There was an Old Person of Rhodes,
Who strongly objected to toads;
He paid several cousins
To catch them by dozens,
That futile Old Person of Rhodes.

There was an Old Man of Peru,
Who watched his wife making a stew;
But once by mistake,
In a stove she did bake
That unfortunate Man of Peru.

There was an Old Man of Melrose,
Who walked on the tips of his toes;
But they said, "It ain't pleasant
To see you at present,
You stupid Old Man of Melrose."

There was a Young Lady of Lucca,
Whose lovers completely forsook her;
She ran up a tree,
And said, "Fiddle-de-dee!"
Which embarrassed the people of Lucca.

There was an Old Man of Bohemia,
Whose daughter was christened Euphemia;
  Till one day, to his grief,
  She married a thief,
Which grieved that Old Man of Bohemia.

There was an Old Man of Vesuvius,
Who studied the works of Vitruvius;
  When the flames burnt his book,
  To drinking he took,
That morbid Old Man of Vesuvius.

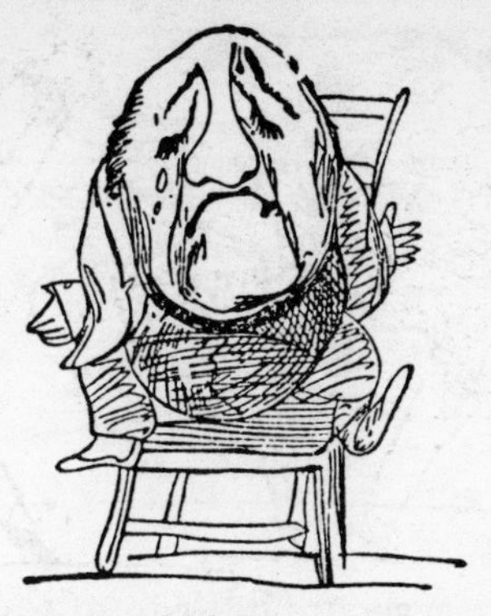

There was an Old Man of Cape Horn,
Who wished he had never been born;
So he sat on a chair,
Till he died of despair,
That dolorous Man of Cape Horn.

There was an Old Lady whose folly
Induced her to sit in a holly;
Whereon by a thorn,
Her dress being torn,
She quickly became melancholy.

There was an Old Man of Corfu,
Who never knew what he should do;
So he rushed up and down,
Till the sun made him brown,
That bewildered Old Man of Corfu.

There was an Old Man of the South,
Who had an immoderate mouth;
But in swallowing a dish,
That was quite full of fish,
He was choked, that Old Man of the South.

There was an Old Man of the Nile,
Who sharpened his nails with a file;
  Till he cut off his thumbs,
  And said calmly, "This comes—
Of sharpening one's nails with a file!"

There was an Old Person of Rheims,
Who was troubled with horrible dreams;
  So, to keep him awake,
  They fed him with cake,
Which amused that Old Person of Rheims.

There was an Old Person of Cromer,
Who stood on one leg to read Homer;
When he found he grew stiff,
He jumped over the cliff,
Which concluded that Person of Cromer.

There was an Old Person of Troy,
Whose drink was warm brandy and soy;
Which he took with a spoon,
By the light of the moon,
In sight of the city of Troy.

There was an Old Man of the Dee,
Who was sadly annoyed by a flea;
When he said, "I will scratch it,"—
They gave him a hatchet,
Which grieved that Old Man of the Dee.

There was an Old Man of Dundee,
Who frequented the top of a tree;
When disturbed by the crows,
He abruptly arose,
And exclaimed, "I'll return to Dundee."

There was an Old Person of Tring,
Who embellished his nose with a ring;
He gazed at the moon,
Every evening in June,
That ecstatic Old Person of Tring.

There was an Old Man on some rocks,
Who shut his wife up in a box;
When she said, "Let me out,"
He exclaimed, "Without doubt,
You will pass all your life in that box."

There was an Old Man of Coblenz,
The length of whose legs was immense;
He went with one prance
From Turkey to France,
That surprising Old Man of Coblenz.

There was an Old Man of Calcutta,
Who perpetually ate bread and butter;
Till a great bit of muffin,
On which he was stuffing,
Choked that horrid Old Man of Calcutta.

There was an Old Man in a pew,
Whose waistcoat was spotted with blue;
But he tore it in pieces,
To give to his nieces,—
That cheerful Old Man in a pew.

There was an Old Man who said, "How,—
Shall I flee from this horrible Cow?
I will sit on this stile,
And continue to smile,
Which may soften the heart of that Cow."

There was a Young Lady of Hull,
Who was chased by a virulent Bull;
But she seized on a spade,
And called out, "Who's afraid!"
Which distracted that virulent Bull.

There was an Old Man of Whitehaven,
Who danced a quadrille with a Raven;
But they said, "It's absurd
To encourage this bird!"
So they smashed that Old Man of Whitehaven.

There was an Old Man of Leghorn,
The smallest as ever was born;
But quickly snapt up he
Was once by a puppy,
Who devoured that Old Man of Leghorn.

There was an Old Man of the Hague,
Whose ideas were excessively vague;
He built a balloon,
To examine the moon,
That deluded Old Man of the Hague.

There was an Old Man of Jamaica,
Who suddenly married a Quaker!
But she cried out, "O lack!
I have married a black!"
Which distressed that Old Man of Jamaica.

There was an Old Person of Dutton,
Whose head was so small as a button;
So to make it look big,
He purchased a wig,
And rapidly rushed about Dutton.

There was a Young Lady of Tyre,
Who swept the loud chords of a lyre;
At the sound of each sweep,
She enraptured the deep,
And enchanted the city of Tyre.

There was an Old Man who said, "Hush!
I perceive a young bird in this bush!"
When they said, "Is it small?"
He replied, "Not at all!
It is four times as big as the bush!"

There was an Old Man of the East,
Who gave all his children a feast;
  But they all ate so much,
  And their conduct was such,
That it killed that Old Man of the East.

There was an Old Man of Kamschatka,
Who possessed a remarkably fat cur;
  His gait and his waddle
  Were held as a model
To all the fat dogs in Kamschatka.

There was an Old Man of the Coast,
Who placidly sat on a post;
But when it was cold,
He relinquished his hold,
And called for some hot buttered toast.

There was an Old Person of Bangor,
Whose face was distorted with anger;
He tore off his boots,
And subsisted on roots,
That borascible Person of Bangor.

There was an Old Man with a beard,
Who sat on a horse when he reared;
But they said, "Never mind!
You will fall off behind,
You propitious Old Man with a beard!"

There was an Old Man of the West,
Who never could get any rest;
So they set him to spin
On his nose and his chin,
Which cured that Old Man of the West.

There was an Old Person of Anerley,
Whose conduct was strange and unmannerly;
He rushed down the Strand,
With a Pig in each hand,
But returned in the evening to Anerley.

There was a Young Lady of Troy,
Whom several large flies did annoy;
Some she killed with a thump,
Some she drowned at the pump,
And some she took with her to Troy.

There was an Old Man of Berlin,
Whose form was uncommonly thin;
Till he once, by mistake,
Was mixed up in a cake,
So they baked that Old Man of Berlin.

There was an Old Person of Spain,
Who hated all trouble and pain;
So he sate on a chair,
With his feet in the air,
That umbrageous Old Person of Spain.

There was a Young Lady of Russia,
Who screamed so that no one could hush her;
Her screams were extreme,
No one heard such a scream
As was screamed by that Lady of Russia.

There was an Old Man, who said, "Well!
Will *nobody* answer this bell?
I have pulled day and night,
Till my hair has grown white,
But nobody answers this bell!"

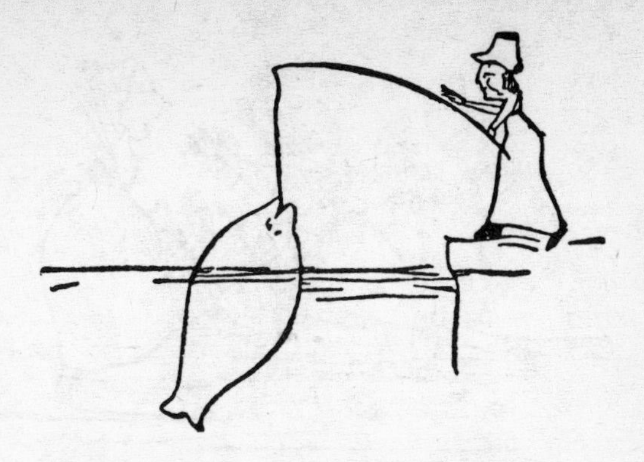

There was a Young Lady of Wales,
Who caught a large fish without scales;
When she lifted her hook,
She exclaimed, "Only look!"
That ecstatic Young Lady of Wales.

There was an Old Person of Cheadle,
Was put in the stocks by the beadle
For stealing some pigs,
Some coats, and some wigs,
That horrible Person of Cheadle.

There was a Young Lady of Welling,
Whose praise all the world was a-telling;
She played on the harp,
And caught several carp,
That accomplished Young Lady of Welling.

There was an Old Person of Tartary,
Who divided his jugular artery;
But he screeched to his wife,
And she said, "Oh, my life!
Your death will be felt by all Tartary!"

There was an Old Person of Chester,
Whom several small children did pester;
They threw some large stones,
Which broke most of his bones,
And displeased that Old Person of Chester.

There was an Old Man with an Owl,
Who continued to bother and howl;
He sate on a rail,
And imbibed bitter ale,
Which refreshed that Old Man and his Owl.

There was an Old Person of Gretna,
Who rushed down the crater of Etna;
When they said, "Is it hot?"
He replied, "No, it's not!"
That mendacious Old Person of Gretna.

There was a Young Lady of Sweden,
Who went by the slow train to Weedon;
When they cried, "Weedon Station!"
She made no observation,
But thought she should go back to Sweden.

There was a Young Girl of Majorca,
Whose aunt was a very fast walker;
She walked seventy miles,
And leaped fifteen stiles,
Which astonished that Girl of Majorca.

There was an Old Man of the Cape,
Who possessed a large Barbary Ape;
Till the Ape one dark night
Set the house on a light,
Which burned that Old Man of the Cape.

There was an Old Lady of Prague,
Whose language was horribly vague:
  When they said, "Are these caps?"
  She answered, "Perhaps!"
That oracular Lady of Prague.

There was an Old Person of Sparta,
Who had twenty-five sons and one daughter;
  He fed them on snails,
  And weighed them in scales,
That wonderful Person of Sparta.

There was an Old Man at a casement,
Who held up his hands in amazement;
When they said, "Sir! you'll fall!"
He replied, "Not at all!"
That incipient Old Man at a casement.

There was an Old Person of Burton,
Whose answers were rather uncertain;
When they said, "How d'ye do?"
He replied, "Who are you?"
That distressing Old Person of Burton.

There was an Old Person of Ems,
Who casually fell in the Thames;
And when he was found,
They said he was drowned,
That unlucky Old Person of Ems.

There was an Old Person of Ewell,
Who chiefly subsisted on gruel;
But to make it more nice,
He inserted some mice,
Which refreshed that Old Person of Ewell.

There was a Young Lady of Parma,
Whose conduct grew calmer and calmer;
When they said, "Are you dumb?"
She merely said, "Hum!"
That provoking Young Lady of Parma.

There was an Old Man of Aôsta,
Who possessed a large Cow, but he lost her;
But they said, "Don't you see,
She has rushed up a tree?
You invidious Old Man of Aôsta!"

There was an Old Man, on whose nose,
Most birds of the air could repose;
But they all flew away,
At the closing of day,
Which relieved that Old Man and his nose.

There was a Young Lady of Clare,
Who was sadly pursued by a bear;
When she found she was tired,
She abruptly expired,
That unfortunate Lady of Clare.

THE JOLLY BEGGAR

& OTHER RHYMES

THE JOLLY BEGGAR

THERE was a jolly beggar,
He had a wooden leg,
Lame from his cradle,
And forced for to beg.
And a-begging we will go,
Will go, will go,
And a-begging we will go.

A bag for his oatmeal,
Another for his salt,
And a long pair of crutches,
To show that he can halt.
And a-begging we will go,
Will go, will go,
And a-begging we will go.

A bag for his wheat,
Another for his rye,
And a little bottle by his side,
To drink when he's a-dry.
And a-begging we will go,
Will go, will go,
And a-begging we will go.

I begg'd for my master,
  And got him store of pelf,
But goodness now be praised,
  I'm begging for myself.
And a-begging we will go,
    Will go, will go,
And a-begging we will go.

In a hollow tree
  I live, and pay no rent,
Providence provides for me,
  And I am well content.
And a-begging we will go,
    Will go, will go,
And a-begging we will go.

Of all the occupations
  A beggar's is the best,
For whenever he's a-weary,
  He can lay him down to rest.
And a-begging we will go,
    Will go, will go,
And a-begging we will go.

I fear no plots against me,
  I live in open cell:
Then who would be a king, lads,
  When the beggar lives so well?
And a-begging we will go,
    Will go, will go,
And a-begging we will go.

THE THREE JOVIAL WELSHMEN

THERE were three jovial Welshmen,
  As I have heard them say,
And they would go a-hunting
  Upon St. David's Day.

All the day they hunted,
  And nothing could they find,
But a ship a-sailing,
  A-sailing with the wind.

One said it was a ship,
  The other he said, nay;
The third said it was a house,
  With the chimney blown away.

And all night they hunted,
  And nothing could they find,
But the moon a-gliding,
  A-gliding with the wind.

One said it was the moon,
  The other he said, nay;
The third said it was a cheese,
  And half o't cut away.

THERE WAS AN OLD WOMAN

THERE was an old woman, as I've heard tell,
She went to market her eggs for to sell;
She went to market all on a market day;
And she fell asleep on the king's highway.

There came by a pedlar whose name was Stout,
He cut her petticoats all round about;
He cut her petticoats up to the knees,
Which made the old woman to shiver and freeze.

When this old woman first did a-wake
She began to shiver and she began to shake.
She began to wonder and she began to cry,
"Lor-a-mercy, Lauk-a-mercy, this is none of I:

"But if it be I, as I do hope it be,
I've a little dog at home, and he'll know me;
If it be I, he'll wag his little tail,
And if it be not I, he'll loudly bark and wail!"

Home went the old woman all in the dark,
Up got her little dog, and he began to bark;
He began to bark, so she began to cry,
"Lor-a-mercy, Lauk-a-mercy, this is none of I!"

KING PIPPIN'S HALL

KING PIPPIN he built a fine new hall,
Pastry and piecrust that was the wall;
The windows were made of black pudding and
white,
Slated with pancakes,—you ne'er saw the like.

PIPPIN HILL

As I went up Pippin Hill,
  Pippin Hill was dirty,
There I met a pretty miss,
  And she dropt me a curtsey.

Little miss, pretty miss,
  Blessings light upon you!
If I had half-a-crown a day
  I'd spend it all on you.

THE CHEAT OF CUPID

One silent night of late,
  When every creature rested,
Came one unto my gate,
  And knocking, me molested.

"Who's that," said I, "beats there,
  And troubles thus the sleepy?"
"Cast off," said he, "all fear,
  And let not locks thus keep ye.

"For I a boy am, who
  By moonless nights have swervèd;
And all with show'rs wet through,
  And e'en with cold half starvèd."

I pitiful arose,
  And soon a taper lighted;
And did myself disclose
  Unto the lad benighted.

I saw he had a bow,
  And wings too, which did shiver;
And looking down below,
  I spied he had a quiver.

I to my chimney's shine
  Brought him, as Love professes,
And chafed his hands with mine,
  And dried his dropping tresses.

But when he felt him warmed,
  "Let's try this bow of ours
And string, if they be harmed,"
  Said he, "with these late show'rs."

Forthwith his bow he bent,
  And wedded string and arrow,
And struck me that it went
  Quite through my heart and marrow.

Then laughing loud, he flew
  Away, and thus said flying,
"Adieu, mine host, adieu,
  I'll leave thy heart a-dying."

LAVENDER'S BLUE

LAVENDER'S blue, Dilly, dilly,
Lavender's green,
When I am king, Dilly, dilly,
You shall be queen.
Call up your men, Dilly, dilly,
Set them to work,
Some to the plough, Dilly, dilly,
Some to the cart;
Some to make hay, Dilly, dilly,
Some to thrash corn;
Whilst you and I, Dilly, dilly,
Keep ourselves warm.

COCK ROBIN'S ROUNDELAY

COCK ROBIN got up early
At the break of day,
And went to Jenny's window
To sing a roundelay.

He sang Cock Robin's love
To the little Jenny Wren,
And when he got unto the end,
Then he began agen.

IN A COTTAGE IN FIFE

In a cottage in Fife
Lived a man and his wife
Who, believe me, were comical folk;
For to people's surprise,
They both saw with their eyes,
And their tongues moved whenever they spoke.

When they were asleep,
I'm told—that to keep
Their eyes open they could not contrive;
They both walked on their feet,
And 'twas thought what they ate,
Help'd, with drinking, to keep them alive.

A FROG HE WOULD A-WOOING GO

A Frog he would a-wooing go,
Heigho, says Rowley,
Whether his mother would let him or no.
With a rowley powley, gammon and spinach,
Heigho, says Anthony Rowley!

So off he set with his opera hat,
Heigho, says Rowley,
And on the road he met with a rat.
With a rowley powley, gammon and spinach,
Heigho, says Anthony Rowley!

"Pray, Mr. Rat, will you go with me,
    Heigho, says Rowley,
Kind Mrs. Mousey for to see?"
    With a rowley powley, gammon and spinach,
    Heigho, says Anthony Rowley!

When they came to the door of Mousey's hall,
    Heigho, says Rowley,
They gave a loud knock and they gave a loud call.
    With a rowley powley, gammon and spinach,
    Heigho, says Anthony Rowley!

"Pray, Mrs. Mouse, are you within?"
    Heigho, says Rowley.
"Oh, yes, kind sirs, I'm sitting to spin."
    With a rowley powley, gammon and spinach,
    Heigho, says Anthony Rowley!

"Pray, Mrs. Mouse, will you give us some beer?
    Heigho, says Rowley,
For Froggy and I are fond of good cheer."
    With a rowley powley, gammon and spinach,
    Heigho, says Anthony Rowley!

"Pray, Mr. Frog, will you give us a song?
    Heigho, says Rowley,
But let it be something that's not very long."
    With a rowley powley, gammon and spinach,
    Heigho, says Anthony Rowley!

"Indeed, Mrs. Mouse," replied the frog,
    Heigho, says Rowley,
"A cold has made me as hoarse as a dog."
    With a rowley powley, gammon and spinach,
    Heigho, says Anthony Rowley!

"Since you have caught cold, Mr. Frog," Mousey said,
Heigho, says Rowley,
"I'll sing you a song that I have just made."
With a rowley powley, gammon and spinach,
Heigho, says Anthony Rowley!

But while they were all a merry-making,
Heigho, says Rowley,
A cat and her kittens came tumbling in.
With a rowley powley, gammon and spinach,
Heigho, says Anthony Rowley!

The cat she seized the rat by the crown;
Heigho, says Rowley,
The kittens they pulled the little mouse down.
With a rowley powley, gammon and spinach,
Heigho, says Anthony Rowley!

This put Mr. Frog in a terrible fright,
Heigho, says Rowley,
He took up his hat, and he wished them good night
With a rowley powley, gammon and spinach,
Heigho, says Anthony Rowley!

But as Froggy was crossing over a brook,
Heigho, says Rowley,
A lily-white duck came and gobbled him up.
With a rowley powley, gammon and spinach,
Heigho, says Anthony Rowley!

So there was an end of one, two, and three,
Heigho, says Rowley,
The Rat, the Mouse, and the little Frog-gee!
With a rowley powley, gammon and spinach,
Heigho, says Anthony Rowley!

NONSENSE RHYMES

from "Alice in Wonderland"

FURY AND THE MOUSE

FURY said to a
mouse, That he
met in the
house,
"Let us
both go
to law:
I will
prosecute
you. Come, I'll
take no denial;
We must
have a trial:
For really
this morning
I've nothing
to do."
Said the
mouse to the
cur, "Such a
trial,
dear Sir,
With no
jury or
judge,
would be
wasting
our breath."
"I'll be judge,
I'll be jury,"
Said
cunning
old Fury:
"I'll
try the
whole
cause,
and
condemn
you
to
death."

HOW DOTH THE LITTLE CROCODILE

How doth the little crocodile
Improve his shining tail,
And pour the waters of the Nile
On every golden scale!

How cheerfully he seems to grin,
How neatly spread his claws,
And welcomes little fishes in
With gently smiling jaws!

YOU ARE OLD, FATHER WILLIAM

"You are old, Father William," the young man said,
"And your hair has become very white;
And yet you incessantly stand on your head—
Do you think, at your age, it is right?"

"In my youth," Father William replied to his son,
"I feared it might injure the brain;
But, now that I'm perfectly sure I have none,
Why, I do it again and again."

"You are old," said the youth, "as I mentioned before,
And have grown most uncommonly fat;
Yet you turned a back-somersault in at the door—
Pray, what is the reason of that?"

"In my youth," said the sage, as he shook his grey
locks,
"I kept all my limbs very supple
By the use of this ointment—one shilling the box—
Allow me to sell you a couple?"

"You are old," said the youth, "and your jaws are
too weak
For anything tougher than suet;
Yet you finished the goose, with the bones and the
beak—
Pray how did you manage to do it?"

"In my youth," said his father, "I took to the law,
And argued each case with my wife;
And the muscular strength, which it gave to my jaw,
Has lasted the rest of my life."

"You are old," said the youth, "one would hardly
suppose
That your eye was as steady as ever;
Yet you balanced an eel on the end of your nose—
What made you so awfully clever?"

"I have answered three questions, and that is
enough,"
Said his father; "don't give yourself airs!
Do you think I can listen all day to such stuff?
Be off, or I'll kick you downstairs!"

SPEAK ROUGHLY TO YOUR LITTLE BOY

SPEAK roughly to your little boy,
And beat him when he sneezes:
He only does it to annoy,
Because he knows it teases.

Chorus

Wow! wow! wow!

I speak severely to my boy,
I beat him when he sneezes;
For he can thoroughly enjoy
The pepper when he pleases!

Chorus

Wow! wow! wow!

TWINKLE, TWINKLE, LITTLE BAT

TWINKLE, twinkle, little bat!
How I wonder what you're at!
Up above the world you fly,
Like a tea-tray in the sky.
Twinkle, twinkle!

WILL YOU WALK A LITTLE FASTER?

"WILL you walk a little faster?" said a whiting to a snail.
"There's a porpoise close behind us, and he's treading on my tail.

See how eagerly the lobsters and the turtles all advance!
They are waiting on the shingle—will you come and join the dance?
Will you, won't you, will you, won't you, will you join the dance?
Will you, won't you, will you, won't you, won't you join the dance?

"You can really have no notion how delightful it will be,
When they take us up and throw us, with the lobsters, out to sea!"
But the snail replied, "Too far, too far!" and gave a look askance—
Said he thanked the whiting kindly, but he would not join the dance.
Would not, could not, would not, could not, would not join the dance.
Would not, could not, would not, could not, could not join the dance.

"What matters it how far we go?" his scaly friend replied.
"There is another shore, you know, upon the other side.
The farther off from England the nearer is to France—
Then turn not pale, beloved snail, but come and join the dance.
Will you, won't you, will you, won't you, will you join the dance?
Will you, won't you, will you, won't you, won't you join the dance?"

'TIS THE VOICE OF THE LOBSTER

'Tis the voice of the Lobster; I heard him declare,
"You have baked me too brown, I must sugar my
hair."
As a duck with its eyelids, so he with his nose
Trims his belt and his buttons, and turns out his toes
When the sands are all dry, he is gay as a lark,
And will talk in contemptuous tones of the Shark:
But, when the tide rises and sharks are around,
His voice has a timid and tremulous sound.

BEAUTIFUL SOUP

Beautiful Soup, so rich and green,
Waiting in a hot tureen!
Who for such dainties would not stoop?
Soup of the evening, beautiful Soup!
Soup of the evening, beautiful Soup!
Beau—ootiful Soo—oop!
Beau—ootiful Soo—oop!
Soo—oop of the e—e—evening,
Beautiful, beautiful Soup!

Beautiful Soup! Who cares for fish,
Game, or any other dish?
Who would not give all else for two p
ennyworth only of beautiful Soup?
Pennyworth only of beautiful Soup?
Beau—ootiful Soo—oop!
Beau—ootiful Soo—oop!
Soo—oop of the e—e—evening,
Beautiful, beauti—FUL SOUP!

THE QUEEN OF HEARTS

The Queen of Hearts, she made some tarts,
All on a summer day:
The Knave of Hearts, he stole those tarts,
And took them quite away!

THEY TOLD ME YOU HAD BEEN TO HER

They told me you had been to her,
And mentioned me to him:
She gave me a good character,
But said I could not swim.

He sent them word I had not gone
(We know it to be true):
If she should push the matter on,
What would become of you?

I gave her one, they gave him two,
You gave us three or more;
They all returned from him to you,
Though they were mine before.

If I or she should chance to be
Involved in this affair,
He trusts to you to set them free,
Exactly as we were.

My notion was that you had been
  (Before she had this fit)
An obstacle that came betweer
  Him, and ourselves, and it.

Don't let him know she liked them best,
  For this must ever be
A secret, kept from all the rest,
  Between yourself and me.

STALKY JACK
AND OTHER RHYMES
from "Lilliput Levee"

STALKY JACK

I KNEW a boy who took long walks,
Who lived on beans and ate the stalks;
To the Giants' Country he lost his way;
They kept him there for a year and a day.
But he has not been the same boy since;
An alteration he did evince;
For you may suppose that he underwent
A change in his notions of extent!

He looks with contempt on a nice high door,
And tries to walk in at the second floor;
He stares with surprise at a basin of soup,
He fancies a bowl as large as a hoop;
He calls the people minikin mites;
He calls a sirloin a couple of bites!
Things having come to these pretty passes,
They bought him some magnifying glasses.

He put on the goggles, and said, "My eyes!
The world has come to its proper size!"
But all the boys cry, "Stalky John!
There you go with your goggles on!"
What girl would marry him—and *quite* right—
To be taken for three times her proper height?
So this comes of taking extravagant walks,
And living on beans, and eating the stalks.

CUCKOO IN THE PEAR-TREE

The Cuckoo sat in the old pear-tree.
Cuckoo!
Raining or snowing, naught cared he.
Cuckoo!
Cuckoo, cuckoo, naught cared he.

The Cuckoo flew over a housetop nigh.
Cuckoo!
"Dear, are you at home, for here am I?
Cuckoo!
Cuckoo, cuckoo, here am I."

"I dare not open the door to you.
Cuckoo!
Perhaps you are not the right cuckoo?
Cuckoo!
Cuckoo, cuckoo, the right Cuckoo!"

"I am the right Cuckoo, the proper one,
Cuckoo!
For I am my father's only son,
Cuckoo!
Cuckoo, cuckoo, his only son."

"If you are your father's only son—
Cuckoo!
The bobbin pull tightly,
Come through the door lightly—
Cuckoo!

If you are your father's only son—
Cuckoo!
It must be you, the only one—
Cuckoo, cuckoo, my own Cuckoo!
Cuckoo!"

TOPSYTURVEY-WORLD

If the butterfly courted the bee,
And the owl the porcupine;
If churches were built in the sea,
And three times one was nine;
If the pony rode his master,
If the buttercups ate the cows,
If the cat had the dire disaster
To be worried, sir, by the mouse;
If mamma, sir, sold the baby
To a gipsy for half a crown;
If a gentleman, sir, was a lady,—
The world would be Upside-Down!
If any or all of these wonders
Should ever come about,
I should not consider them blunders,
For I should be Inside-Out!

Chorus

Ba-ba, black wool,
Have you any sheep?
Yes, sir, a pack-full,
Creep, mouse, creep!
Four-and-twenty little maids
Hanging out the pie,

Out jumped the honey-pot,
  Guy-Fawkes, Guy!
Cross-latch, cross-latch,
  Sit and spin the fire,
When the pie was opened,
  The bird was on the brier!

FRODGEDOBBULUM'S FANCY

I

Did you ever see Giant Frodgedobbulum,
With his double great-toe and his double great
    thumb?

Did you ever hear Giant Frodgedobbulum
Saying *Fa-fe-fi*, and *Fo-faw-fum*?

He shakes the earth as he walks along,
As deep as the sea, as far as Hong-Kong!

He is a giant, and no mistake;
With teeth like the prongs of a garden rake!

II

The Giant Frodgedobbulum got out of bed,
Sighing, "Heigh-ho! that I were but wed!"

The Giant Frodgedobbulum sat in his chair,
Saying, "Why should a giant be wanting a fair?"

The Giant Frodgedobbulum said to his boots,
"The first maid I meet I will wed, if she suits!"

They were Magic Boots, and they laughed as he
spoke—
"Oh ho," says the giant, "you think it's a joke?"

III

So he put on his boots, and came stumping down,
Clatter and clump, into Banbury town—

He did not fly into Banbury,
For plenty of time to walk had he!

He kicked at the gate—"Within there, ho!"
"Oh, what is your name?" says the porter Slow.

"Oh, the Giant Frodgedobbulum am I,
For a wife out of Banbury town I sigh!"

Up spake the porter, bold and free,
"Your room we prefer to your company."

Up spake Frodgedobbulum, free and bold,
"I will build up your town with silver and gold!"

Up spake Marjorie, soft and small,
"I will not be your wife at all!"

The giant knocked in the gate with his feet,
And there stood Marjorie in the street!

She was nine years old, she was lissome and fair,
And she wore emeralds in her hair.

She could dance like a leaf, she could sing like a
thrush,
She was bold as the north wind, and sweet as a blush.

Her father tanned, her mother span,
"But Marjorie shall marry a gentleman,—

Silks and satins, I'll lay you a crown!"—
So said the people in Banbury town.

Such was Marjorie—and who should come
To woo her but this Frodgedobbulum,

A vulgar giant, who wore no gloves,
And very pig-headed in his loves!

IV

They rang the alarum, and in the steeple
They tolled the church-bells to rouse the people.

But all the people in Banbury town
Could not put Frodgedobbulum down.

The tanner thought to stab him dead—
"Somebody pricked me!" the giant said.

The mother wept—"I do not care,"
Said F.—"Why should I be wanting a fair?"

He snatched up Marjorie, stroked his boot,
And fled; with Banbury in pursuit!

"What ho, my boots! put forth your power!
Carry me sixty miles an hour!"

In ditches and dikes, over stocks and stones,
The Banbury people fell, with groans.

Frodgedobbulum passed over river and tree,
Gollopy-gallop, with Marjorie;—

The people beneath her Marjorie sees
Of the size of mites in an Oxford cheese!

V

Castle Frodgedobbulum sulked between
Two bleak hills, in a deep ravine.

It was always dark there, and always drear,
The same time of day and the same time of year.

The walls of the castle were slimy and black,
There were dragons in front, and toads at the back.

Spiders there were, and of vampires lots;
Ravens croaked round the chimney-pots.

Seven bulldogs barked in the hall;
Seven wild-cats did caterwaul!

The giant said, with a smirk on his face,
"My Marjorie, this is a pretty place;

As Mrs. F. you will lead, with me,
A happier life than in Banbury!

Pour out my wine, and comb my hair,
And let me to sleep in my easy chair;

But, first, my boots I will kick away."—
And Marjorie answered, "*S'il vous plait!*"

Then the giant mused, "It befits my station
To marry a lady of education;

But who would have thought this Banbury wench
Was so accomplished, and could speak French?"

Did you ever hear Frodgedobbulum snore?
He shook the castle from roof to floor!

Fast asleep as a pig was he—
"And very much like one!" thought Marjorie.

VI

Then Marjorie stood on a leathern chair,
And opened the window to the air.

The bats flap, the owls hoot—
Marjorie lifted the giant's boot!

The ravens shriek, the owls hoot—
Marjorie got into the giant's boot!

And Marjorie said, "I can reach the moon
Before you waken, you big buffoon!"

Once, twice, three times, and away,—
"Which is the road to Banbury, pray?"

The Boot made answer, "Hah, hah! hoh, hoh!
The road to Banbury town I know."

VII

The giant awoke in his easy chair,
Saying, "Ho, little Marjorie, are you there?

A stoup of wine, to be spiced the same!—
Exquisite Marjorie, *je vous aime*!"

Now where was Marjorie? Safe and sound
In the Magic Boot she cleared the ground.

Frodgedobbulum groaned—"I am bereft!
The left boot's gone, and the right is left!—

The window's open! I'll bet a crown
The chit is off to Banbury town!

But follow, follow, my faithful Boot!
One is enough for the pursuit;

And back to my arms the wench shall come
As sure as my name's Frodgedobbulum!"

VIII

Hasty Frodgedobbulum, being a fool,
Forgot of the Magic Boots the rule.

They were made on a right and a left boot-tree,
But he put the wrong leg in the boot, you see!

It was a terrible mistake
For even a giant in love to make—

Terrible in its consequences,
Frightful to any man's seven senses!

Down came a thunderbolt, rumble and glare!
Frodgedobbulum Castle blew up in the air!

The giant, deprived of self-control,
Was carried away to the very North Pole;

For such was the magic rule. Poor F.
Now sits on the peak of the Arctic cliff!

The point is so sharp it makes him shrink;
The northern streamers, they make him blink;

One boot on, and one boot off,
He shivers, and shakes, and thinks, with a cough:

"Safe in Banbury Marjorie dwells;
Marjorie will marry someone else!".

IX

And so Frodgedobbulum, the giant,
Sits on the North Pole incompliant.

He blinks at the snow with its weary white;
He blinks at the spears of the northern light;

Kicks out with one boot; says, "Fi-fo-fum!
I am the Giant Frodgedobbulum!"

But who cares whether he is or not,
Living in such an inclement spot?

Banbury town is the place for me,
And a kiss from merry Marjorie,

With the clerk in the vestry to see all fair—
For she wears orange-flowers in her hair!

She can dance like a leaf, she can sing like a thrush,
She is bold as the north wind, and sweet as a blush;

Her father he tans, her mother she spins;
Frodgedobbulum sits on the Pole for his sins;

But here comes Marjorie, white as milk,
A rose on her bosom as soft as silk,

On her finger a gay gold ring;
The bridegroom holds up his head like a king!

Marjorie has married a gentleman;
Who knows when the wedding began?

SHOCK-HEADED CICELY AND THE TWO BEARS

I

"O YES! O yes! O yes! ding dong!"
The bellman's voice is loud and strong;
So is his bell: "O yes! ding dong!"

He wears a red coat with golden lace;
See how the people of the place
Come running to hear what the bellman says!

"O yes! Sir Nicholas Hildebrand
Has just returned from the Holy Land,
And freely offers his heart and hand—

O yes! O yes! O yes! ding dong!"—
All the women hurry along,
Maids and widows, a chattering throng.

"O sir, you are hard to understand!
To whom does he offer his heart and hand?
Explain your meaning, we do command!"

"O yes! ding dong! you shall understand!
O yes! Sir Nicholas Hildebrand
Invites the ladies of this land

To feast with him in his castle strong
This very day at three. Ding dong!
O yes! O yes! O yes! ding dong!"

Then all the women went off to dress,
Mary, Margaret, Bridget, Bess,
Patty, and more than I can guess.

They powdered their hair with golden dust
And bought new ribbons—they said they must—
But none of them painted, we will trust.

Long before the time arrives,
All the women that could be wives
Are dressed within an inch of their lives.

Meanwhile, Sir Nicholas Hildebrand
Had brought with him from the Holy Land
A couple of bears—oh, that was grand!

He tamed the bears, and they loved him true,
Whatever he told them they would do—
Hark! 'tis the town clock striking two!

II

Among the maidens of low degree
The poorest of all was Cicely—
A shabbier girl could hardly be.

"Oh, I should like to see the feast,
But my frock is old, my shoes are pieced,
My hair is rough!"—(it never was greased).

The clock struck three! She durst not go!
But she heard the band, and to see the show,
Crept after the people that went in a row.

When Cicely came to the castle gate
The porter exclaimed, "Miss Shaggy-pate,
The hall is full, and you come too late!"

Just then the music made a din,
Flute, and cymbal, and culverin,
And Cicely, with a squeeze, got in!

Oh, what a sight! full fifty score
Of dames that Cicely knew, and more,
Filling the hall from dais to door!

The dresses were like a garden-bed,
Green and gold, and blue and red—
Poor Cicely thought of her tossy head!

She heard the singing—she heard the clatter—
Clang of flagon, and clink of platter—
But, oh, the feast was no such matter!

For she saw Sir Nicholas himself,
Raised on a dais just like a shelf,
And fell in love with him—shabby elf!

Her heart beat quick, aside she stept;
Under the tapestry she crept,
Tousling her tossy hair, and wept!

Her cheeks were wet, her eyes were red—
"Who makes that noise?" the ladies said;
"Turn out that girl with the shaggy head!"

III

Just then there was heard a double roar,
That shook the place, both wall and floor;
Everybody looked to the door.

It was a roar, it was a growl;
The ladies set up a little howl,
And flapped and clucked like frightened fowl.

Sir Hildebrand for silence begs—
In walk the bears on their hinder legs,
Wise as owls, and merry as grigs!

The dark girls tore their hair of sable;
The fair girls hid underneath the table;
Some fainted; to move they were not able.

But most of them could scream and screech—
Sir Nicholas Hildebrand made a speech:
"Order! ladies, I do beseech!"

The bears looked hard at Cicely
Because her hair hung wild and free—
"Related to us, miss, you must be!"

Then Cicely, filling two plates of gold
As full of cherries as they could hold,
Walked up to the bears, and spoke out bold.

"Welcome to you! and to *you*, Mr. Bear!
Will you take a chair? will *you* take a chair?
This is an honour, we do declare!"

Sir Hildebrand strode up to see,
Saying, "Who may this maiden be?
Ladies, this is the wife for me!"

Almost before they could understand,
He took up Cicely by the hand,
And danced with her a saraband.

Her hair was as rough as a parlour broom,
It swung, it swirled all round the room—
Those ladies were vexed, we may presume.

Sir Nicholas kissed her on the face,
And set her beside him on the dais,
And made her the lady of the place.

The nuptials soon they did prepare,
With a silver comb for Cicely's hair:
There were bands of music everywhere.

And in that beautiful bridal show
Both the bears were seen to go
Upon their hind legs to and fro!

Now every year on the wedding-day
The boys and girls come out to play,
And scramble for cherries as they may,

With a cheer for this and the other bear,
And a cheer for Sir Nicholas, free and fair,
And a cheer for Cis, of the tossy hair—

With one cheer more (if you will wait)
For every girl with a curly pate
Who keeps her hair in a proper state.

Sing bear's grease! curling-irons to sell!
Sing combs and brushes! sing tortoise-shell!
O yes! ding dong! the crier, the bell!
—Isn't this a pretty tale to tell?

THE DREAM OF A BOY WHO LIVED AT NINE-ELMS

Nine grenadiers, with bayonets in their guns;
Nine bakers' baskets, with hot-cross buns;
Nine brown elephants, standing in a row;
Nine new velocipedes, good ones to go;
Nine knickerbocker suits, with buttons all complete;
Nine pair of skates with straps for the feet;
Nine clever conjurers eating hot coals;
Nine sturdy mountaineers leaping on their poles;
Nine little drummer-boys beating on their drums;
Nine fat aldermen sitting on their thumbs;
Nine new knockers to our front door;
Nine new neighbours that I never saw before;
Nine times running I dreamt it all plain;
With bread and cheese for supper I could dream it
all again!

THE DREAM OF A GIRL WHO LIVED AT SEVEN-OAKS

SEVEN sweet singing birds up in a tree;
Seven swift sailing-ships white upon the sea;
Seven bright weather-cocks shining in the sun;
Seven slim race-horses ready for a run;
Seven gold butterflies, flitting overhead;
Seven red roses blowing in a garden bed;
Seven white lilies, with honey bees inside them;
Seven round rainbows with clouds to divide them;
Seven pretty little girls with sugar on their lips;
Seven witty little boys, whom everybody tips;
Seven nice fathers, to call little maids joys;
Seven nice mothers, to kiss the little boys;
Seven nights running I dreamt it all plain;
With bread and jam for supper I could dream it
all again!

THE PEDLAR'S CARAVAN

I WISH I lived in a caravan,
With a horse to drive, like the pedlar-man!
Where he comes from nobody knows,
Or where he goes to, but on he goes!

His caravan has windows two,
And a chimney of tin, that the smoke comes through;
He has a wife, with a baby brown,
And they go riding from town to town.

Chairs to mend, and delf to sell!
He clashes the basins like a bell;
Tea-trays, baskets ranged in order,
Plates, with the alphabet round the border!

The roads are brown, and the sea is green,
But his house is just like a bathing-machine;
The world is round, and he can ride,
Rumble and splash, to the other side!

With the pedlar-man I should like to roam,
And write a book when I came home;
All the people would read my book,
Just like the Travels of Captain Cook!

CLEAN CLARA

What! not know our Clean Clara?
Why, the hot folks in Sahara,
And the cold Esquimaux,
Our little Clara know!
Clean Clara, the Poet sings,
Cleaned a hundred thousand things!

She cleaned the keys of the harpsichord,
She cleaned the hilt of the family sword,
She cleaned my lady, she cleaned my lord;
All the pictures in their frames,
Knights with daggers, and stomachered dames—
Cecils, Godfreys, Montforts, Græmes,
Winifreds—all those nice old names!

She cleaned the works of the eight-day clock,
She cleaned the spring of a secret lock,
She cleaned the mirror, she cleaned the cupboard;
All the books she india-rubbered!

She cleaned the Dutch-tiles in the place,
She cleaned some very old-fashioned lace;
The Countess of Miniver came to her,
"Pray, my dear, will you clean my fur?"
All her cleanings are admirable;
To count your teeth you will be able,
If you look in the walnut-table!

She cleaned the tent-stitch and the sampler;
She cleaned the tapestry, which was ampler;
Joseph going down into the pit,
And the Shunammite woman with the boy in a fit;

You saw the reapers, *not* in the distance,
And Elisha coming to the child's assistance,
With the house on the wall that was built for the
prophet,
The chair, the bed, and the bolster of it;

The eyebrows all had a twirl reflective,
Just like an eel: to spare invective,
There was plenty of colour, but no perspective.
However, Clara cleaned it all,
With a curious lamp, that hangs in the hall;
She cleaned the drops of the chandeliers,
Madam in mittens was moved to tears!

She cleaned the cage of the cockatoo,
The oldest bird that ever grew;

I should say a thousand years old would do—
I'm sure he looked it; but nobody knew;
She cleaned the china, she cleaned the delf,
She cleaned the baby, she cleaned herself!

To-morrow morning she means to try
To clean the cobwebs from the sky;
Some people say the girl will rue it,
But my belief is she will do it.

So I've made up my mind to be there to see:
There's a beautiful place in the walnut-tree;
The bough is as firm as the solid rock;
She brings out her broom at six o'clock.

THE

English Struwwelpeter

OR PRETTY STORIES AND FUNNY PICTURES

♣ ♣ ♣

WHEN the children have been good,
That is, be it understood,
Good at meal-times, good at play,
Good all night, and good all day,—
They shall have the pretty things
Merry Christmas always brings.
Naughty, romping girls and boys,
Tear their clothes and make a noise,
Spoil their pinafores and frocks,
And deserve no Christmas-box,
Such as these shall never look
At this pretty Picture-Book.

1. SHOCK-HEADED PETER

SHOCK-HEADED Peter! There he stands,
With his horrid hair and hands.
Peter's nails are never cut;
They are grim'd as black as soot;
Dirty boy, I do declare,
He has never comb'd his hair;
If he did, would he be sweeter?
He'd still be Shock-headed Peter.

2. THE STORY OF CRUEL FREDERICK

HERE is cruel Frederick, see!
A horrid wicked boy was he;
He caught the flies, poor little things,
And then tore off their tiny wings,
He kill'd the birds, and broke the chairs,
And threw the kitten down the stairs,
And oh! far worse than all beside,
He whipp'd poor Mary, till she cried.

The trough was full, and faithful Tray
Came out to drink one sultry day;

He wagg'd his tail,
and wet his lip,
When cruel Fred snatch'd up
a whip,
And whipp'd poor Tray till he
was sore,
And kick'd and
whipp'd him
more and more.

At this, good Tray grew very red,
And growl'd and bit him till he bled;
Then you should only have been by,
To see how Fred did scream and cry!

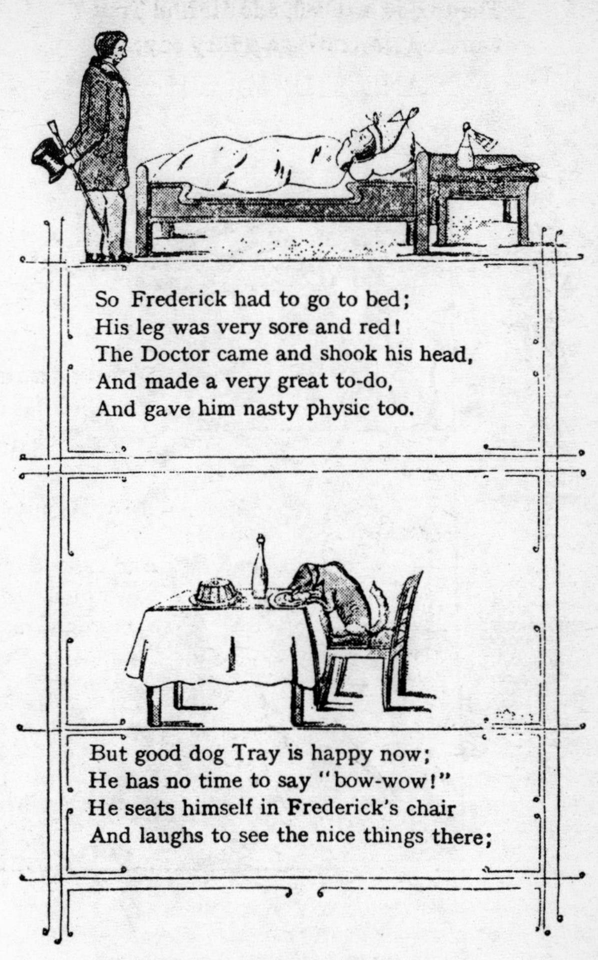

So Frederick had to go to bed;
His leg was very sore and red!
The Doctor came and shook his head,
And made a very great to-do,
And gave him nasty physic too.

But good dog Tray is happy now;
He has no time to say "bow-wow!"
He seats himself in Frederick's chair
And laughs to see the nice things there;

The soup he swallows, sup by sup,—
And eats the pies and puddings up.

3. THE DREADFUL STORY ABOUT HARRIET AND THE MATCHES

IT almost makes me cry to tell
What foolish Harriet befell.

Mamma and Nurse went out one day
And left her all alone at play;
Now, on the table close at hand,
A box of matches chanc'd to stand;
And kind Mamma and Nurse had told her,
That, if she touch'd them, they should scold her
But Harriet said: "Oh, what a pity!
For, when they burn, it is so pretty;
They crackle so, and spit, and flame;
Mamma, too, often does the same."

The pussy-cats heard this,
And they began to hiss,
And stretch their claws
And raise their paws;
"Me-ow," they said, "me-ow, me-o,
You'll burn to death, if you do so."

But Harriet would not take advice,
She lit a match, it was so nice!
It crackled so, it burn'd so clear,—
Exactly like the picture here.
She jump'd for joy and ran about
And was too pleas'd to put it out.

The pussy-cats saw this
And said: "Oh, naughty, naughty Miss!"

And stretch'd their claws
And rais'd their paws:

"'Tis very, very wrong, you know,
Me-ow, mee-o, me-ow, me-o,
You will be burnt, if you do so."

And see! Oh! what a dreadful thing!
The fire has caught her apron-string;
Her apron burns, her arms, her hair;
She burns all over, everywhere.

Then how the pussy-cats did mew,
What else, poor pussies, could they do?
They scream'd for help, 'twas all in vain!
So then they said: "We'll scream again;
Make haste, make haste, me-ow, me-o,
She'll burn to death, we told her so."

So she was burnt, with all her clothes,
And arms, and hands, and eyes, and nose;
Till she had nothing more to lose
Except her little scarlet shoes;
And nothing else but these was found
Among her ashes on the ground.

And when the good cats sat beside
The smoking ashes, how they cried!
"Me-ow, me-oo, me-ow, me-oo,
What will Mamma and Nursy do?"
Their tears ran down their cheeks so fast;
They made a little pond at last.

4. THE STORY OF THE INKY BOYS

As he had often done before,
The woolly-headed black-a-moor
One nice fine summer's day went out
To see the shops and walk about;
And as he found it hot,
poor fellow,
He took with him his green
umbrella.
Then Edward, little noisy
wag,
Ran out and laugh'd, and
wav'd his flag;
And William came in jacket
trim
And brought his wooden hoop with him;
And Arthur, too, snatch'd up his toys
And join'd the other naughty boys;

So, one and all set up
a roar
And laugh'd and hoot-
ed more and more,
And kept on singing,
—only think!—
"Oh! Blacky, you're
as black as ink."

Now tall Agrippa lived close by,—
So tall, he almost touch'd the sky;
He had a mighty inkstand too,
In which a great goose-feather grew;
He call'd out in an angry tone:
"Boys, leave the black-a-moor alone;

For if he tries with all his might,
He cannot change from black to white."
But ah! they did not mind a bit
What great Agrippa said of it;
But went on laughing as before,
And hooting at the black-a-moor.

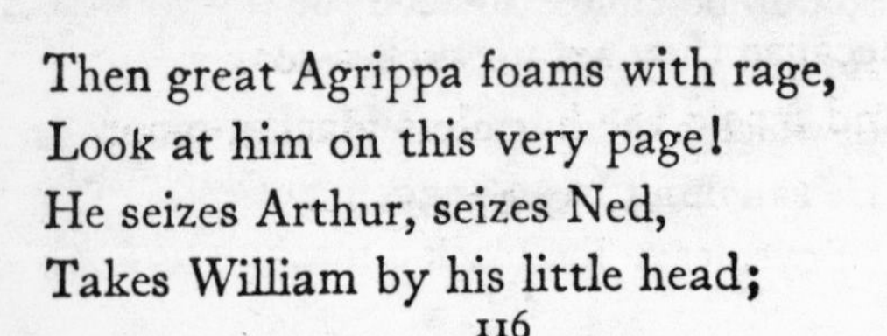

Then great Agrippa foams with rage,
Look at him on this very page!
He seizes Arthur, seizes Ned,
Takes William by his little head;

And they may scream and kick and call,
Into the ink he dips them all;
Into the inkstand, one, two, three,
Till they are black, as black can be;
Look up! look up! and you shall see.
Ah! there they are, and there they run!
The black-a-moor enjoys the fun.
They have been made as black as crows,
Quite black all over, eyes and nose,
And legs, and arms, and heads, and toes,
And trousers, pinafores, and toys,—
The silly little inky boys!
Because they set up such a roar,
And teas'd the harmless black-a-moor.

5. THE STORY OF THE MAN THAT WENT OUT SHOOTING

THIS is the man that shoots the hares;
This is the coat he always wears:
With game-bag, powder-
horn and gun
He's going out to have
some fun.

The hare sits
snug in leaves
and grass,
And laughs to see
the green man
pass.

He finds it hard, without a pair
Of spectacles, to shoot the hare.

Now, as the sun grew very hot,
And he a heavy gun had got,
He lay down underneath
a tree
And went to sleep,
as you
may see.

And, while he slept like any top,
The little hare came, hop, hop, hop,
Took gun and spectacles, and then
On her hind legs went off again.

The green man wakes and sees her place
The spectacles upon her face;
And now she's trying all she can
To shoot the sleepy, green-coat man.
He cries and screams and runs away;
The hare runs after him all day,
And hears him call out everywhere:
"Help! Fire! Help! The Hare! The Hare!"

At last he stumbled at the well
Head over ears, and in he fell.

The hare stopp'd short, took aim, and hark!
Bang went the gun,—she miss'd her mark!
The poor man's wife was drinking up
Her coffee in her coffee-cup;
The gun shot cup and saucer through;
"O dear!" cried she, "what shall I do?"
There liv'd close by the cottage there
The hare's own child, the little hare;
And while she stood upon her toes,
The coffee fell and burn'd her nose.
"O dear!" she cried, with spoon in hand,
"Such fun I do not understand."

6. THE STORY OF LITTLE SUCK-A-THUMB

ONE day, Mamma said: "Conrad dear,
I must go out and leave you here.
But mind now, Conrad, what I say,
Don't suck your thumb while I'm away.
The great tall tailor always comes
To little boys that suck their thumbs,
And ere they dream what he's about,
He takes his great sharp scissors out
And cuts their thumbs clean off,—and then,
You know, they never grow again."

Mamma had scarcely turn'd her back,
The thumb was in, Alack! Alack!

The door flew open, in he ran,
The great, long, red-legg'd scissor-
man.
Oh! children, see! the tailor's
come
And caught out little Suck-a-
Thumb.
Snip! Snap! Snip! the scissors go;
And Conrad cries out—Oh! Oh!
Oh!
Snip! Snap! Snip! They go so fast,
That both his thumbs are off at
last.

Mamma comes home; there Conrad stands,
And looks quite sad, and shows his hands,—
"Ah!" said Mamma, "I knew he'd come
To naughty little Suck-a-Thumb."

7. THE STORY OF AUGUSTUS WHO WOULD NOT HAVE ANY SOUP

AUGUSTUS was a chubby lad;
Fat ruddy cheeks Augustus had;
And everybody saw with joy
The plump and hearty healthy boy.
He ate and drank as he was told,
And never let his soup get cold.
But one day, one cold winter's day,
He scream'd out—"Take the soup away!
O take the nasty soup away
I won't have any soup to-day."

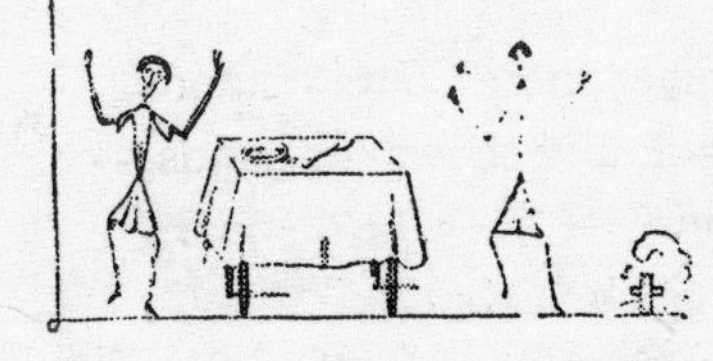

Next day, now look, the picture shows
How lank and lean Augustus grows!

Yet, though he feels so weak and ill,
The naughty fellow cries out still—
"Not any soup for me, I say:
O take the nasty soup away!
I won't have any soup to-day."

The third day comes; O what a sin
To make himself so pale and thin!
Yet, when the soup is put on table,
He screams, as loud as he is able—
"Not any soup for me, I say:
O take the nasty soup away!
I won't have any soup to-day."

Look at him, now the fourth day's come!
He scarcely weighs a sugar-plum;
He's like a little bit of thread;
And on the fifth day, he was—dead!

8. THE STORY OF FIDGETY PHILIP

Let me see if Philip can
Be a little gentleman;
Let me see if he is able
To sit still for once at table:
Thus Papa bade Phil behave;
And Mamma look'd very
But fidgety Phil, [grave.
He won't sit still;
He wriggles
And giggles,

And then, I declare,
Swings backwards and forwards
And tilts up his chair,
Just like any rocking-horse;—
"Philip! I am getting cross!"

See the naughty restless child
Growing still more rude and wild,
Till his chair falls over quite.
Philip screams with all his might,
Catches at the cloth, but then
That makes matters worse again.
Down upon the ground they fall,
Glasses, plates, knives, forks and all.

How Mamma did fret and frown,
When she saw them tumbling down!
And Papa made such a face!
Philip is in sad disgrace.

Where is Philip, where is he?
Fairly cover'd up, you see!
Cloth and all are lying on him;
He has pull'd down all upon
What a terrible to-do! [him.
Dishes, glasses, snapt in two!
Here a knife, and there a fork!
Philip, this is cruel work.

Table all so bare, and ah!
Poor Papa and poor Mamma
Look quite cross, and wonder how
They shall make their dinner now.

9. THE STORY OF JOHNNY HEAD-IN-AIR

As he trudg'd along to school,
It was always Johnny's rule
To be looking at the sky
And the clouds that floated by;
But what just before him lay,
In his way,
Johnny never thought about;
So that everyone cried out—
"Look at little Johnny there,
Little Johnny Head-in-Air!"

Running just in Johnny's way,
Came a little dog one day;
Johnny's eyes were still astray

Up on high,
In the sky;
And he never heard them cry—
"Johnny, mind, the dog is nigh!"
Bump!
Dump!
Down they fell, with such a thump,
Dog and Johnny in a lump!

Once, with head as high as ever,
Johnny walk'd beside the river.
Johnny watch'd the swallows trying
Which was cleverest at flying.
Oh! what fun!
Johnny watch'd the bright round sun
Going in and coming out;
This was all he thought about.
So he strode on, only think!
To the river's very brink,
Where the bank was high and steep,
And the water very deep;
And the fishes, in a row,
Stared to see him coming so.

One step more! Oh! sad to tell!
Headlong in poor Johnny fell.
And the fishes, in dismay,
Wagg'd their tails and ran away.
There lay Johnny on his face,
With his nice red writing-case;
But, as they were passing by,
Two strong men had heard him cry;
And, with sticks, these two strong men
Hook'd poor Johnny out again.

Oh! you should have seen him shiver
When they pull'd him from the river.
He was in a sorry plight!
Dripping wet, and such a fright!
Wet all over, everywhere,
Clothes, and arms, and face, and hair:
Johnny never will forget
What it is to be so wet.

And the fishes, one, two, three,
Are come back again, you see;
Up they came the moment after,
To enjoy the fun and laughter.
Each popp'd out his little head,
And, to tease poor Johnny, said:
"Silly little Johnny, look,
You have lost your writing-book!"

10. THE STORY OF FLYING ROBERT

WHEN the rain comes tumbling down
In the country or the town,
All good little girls and boys
Stay at home and mind their toys.

Robert thought,—"No, when it pours,
It is better out of doors."
Rain it *did*, and in a minute
Bob was in it.

Here you see him, silly fellow,
Underneath his red umbrella.

What a wind! Oh! how it whistles
Through the trees and flow'rs and thistles!
It has caught his red umbrella;
Now look at him, silly fellow,

Up he flies
To the skies.
No one heard his screams and cries,
Through the clouds the rude wind bore him,
And his hat flew on before him.
Soon they got to such a height,
They were nearly out of sight!
And the hat went up so high,
That it really touch'd the sky.
No one ever yet could tell
Where they stopp'd, or where they fell:
Only, this one thing is plain,
Bob was never seen again!

NONSENSE TALES

BARON MUNCHAUSEN'S WONDERFUL HORSE

When I was at Count Przobossky's noble country-seat in Lithuania, one day I was with the ladies at tea in the drawing-room, while the gentlemen were down in the yard, to see a young horse of blood which had just arrived from the stud. We suddenly heard a noise of distress. I hastened downstairs, and found the horse so unruly, that nobody durst approach or mount him. The most resolute horsemen stood dismayed and aghast; despondency was expressed in every countenance, when, in one leap, I was on his back, took him by surprise, and worked him quite into gentleness and obedience, with the best display of horsemanship I was master of. Fully to show this to the ladies, and save them unnecessary trouble, I forced him to leap in at one of the open windows of the tea-room, walked round several times, pace, trot, and gallop, and at last made him mount the tea-table, there to repeat his lessons in a pretty style of miniature which was exceedingly pleasing to the ladies, for he performed them amazingly well, and did not break either cup or saucer. It placed me so high in their opinion, and so well in that of the noble lord, that, with his usual politeness, he begged I would accept of this young horse, and ride him full career to conquest and honour in the campaign against the Turks, which was soon to be opened, under the command of Count Munich.

I could not indeed have received a more agreeable present, nor a more ominous one at the opening of that campaign, in which I made my apprenticeship as a soldier. A horse so gentle, so spirited, and so fierce—at once a lamb and a lion—put me always in mind of the soldier's duty! of young Alexander, and of the astonishing things he performed in the field.

We took the field, among several other reasons, it seems, with an intention to retrieve the character of the Russian arms, which had been blemished a little by Czar Peter's last campaign on the Pruth; and this we fully accomplished by several very fatiguing and glorious campaigns under the command of that great general I mentioned before.

We had very hot work once in the van of the army, when we drove the Turks into Oczakow. My spirited charger had almost brought me into a scrape: I had an advanced fore-post, and saw the enemy coming against me in a cloud of dust, which left me rather uncertain about their actual numbers and real intentions. To wrap myself up in a similar cloud was common prudence, but would not have much advanced my knowledge, or answered the end for which I had been sent out; therefore I let my flankers on both wings spread to the right and left, and make what dust they could, and I myself led on straight upon the enemy, to have a nearer sight of them: in this I was gratified, for they stood and fought, till, for fear of my flankers, they began to move off rather disorderly. This was the moment to fall upon them

THE WATER RAN OUT AS IT CAME IN

with spirit; we broke them entirely—made a terrible havoc amongst them, and drove them not only back to a walled town in their rear, but even through it, contrary to our most sanguine expectation.

The swiftness of my steed enabled me to be foremost in the pursuit; and seeing the enemy fairly flying through the opposite gate, I thought it would be prudent to stop in the market-place, to order the men to rendezvous. I stopped, gentlemen; but judge of my astonishment when in this market-place I saw not one of my hussars about me! Are they scouring the other streets? or what is become of them? They could not be far off, and must, at all events, soon join me. In that expectation I walked my panting charger to a spring in this market-place, and let him drink. He drank uncommonly, with an eagerness not to be satisfied, but natural enough; for when I looked round for my men, what should I see, gentlemen! the hind part of the poor creature, croup and legs, were missing, as if he had been cut in two, and the water ran out as it came in, without refreshing or doing him any good! How it could have happened was quite a mystery to me, till I returned with him to the town-gate. There I saw, that when I rushed in pell-mell with the flying enemy, they had dropped the portcullis (a heavy falling door, with sharp spikes at the bottom, let down suddenly to prevent the entrance of an enemy into a fortified town) unperceived by me, which had totally cut off his hind part, that still lay quivering on the outside of the gate. It would have been an irreparable loss, had not our farrier contrived to bring both parts together while hot. He sewed them up with sprigs and young shoots of laurels that were at hand; the wound healed, and, what could not have happened but to so glorious a horse, the sprigs took root in his body, grew up, and formed a bower over me; so that afterwards I could go upon many other expeditions in the shade of my own and my horse's laurels.

THE STRANGE JOURNEY OF TUFLONGBO

"When I set out on my long journey," said Tuflongbo to the Fairy Queen, "I took the south road through Shineland, meaning to pass by the country of the Picknickers who work in the mines. But I gave that up because a magpie I met foretold ill-luck if I went there, and leaving that route, I turned off to the west, and travelled on till I came to World's End, which is bounded by a high brick wall. When I saw the wall my heart failed me, though at that very moment I was on the very eve of the proudest day of my life! Over the wall grew a stout trailing plant, with a five-peaked glossy leaf, and clusters of dark purple berries; and up it I climbed till I had gained the top, and through tears of joy beheld a strange country stretching beyond. As my eyes grew clear again, imagine my delight at seeing in the plain below me a vast body of men in blue aprons. What do you think they were doing? Cutting up the old Moons and making Stars of them!"

Here Tuflongbo paused, utterly overcome, but the Fairy Queen slapped him on the back and he came to, and continued his tale:

"Yes, a band of men in blue aprons cutting up the old Moons and making Stars of them! I was so lost in wonder that I remained for some hours spell-bound, and watching the process of conversion undiscovered; but at length one of the star-makers threw back his head, opened his mouth in a wide yawn, and I caught his eye. The only thing left for me to do was to bow low and introduce myself as Tuflongbo, the great traveller from Shineland. He laughed and yawned by turns, as he tried to repeat Tuflongbo; and then invited me to make a stay at his house, but I excused myself as I had a long journey to make.

"At that, the moon-cutters all threw their blue aprons over their heads and moaned aloud. So I hurried off as fast as possible, and travelled on till one evening I came to the shores of a vast sea, upon which no sail was to be seen. My heart sank as I paced the shore wondering how to cross the water; but at length I was relieved to see a lanky old man coming along with a bundle of nets in his arms. I began to question him excitedly about this strange sea and its far-off opposite shores. He did not seem to understand at first, but then he replied, that if I crossed the sea I should come to the country of the Applepivi.

"'But how am I to cross it?' I asked him.

"'Cross it? It is only three sights over,' he replied.

"'*Three sights over?*' I repeated. 'Will you be pleased to explain your meaning?'

"'Only this: Stand on the shore, look to the horizon, and jump—that is *one* sight. Pause, look, and jump again—that is *two* sights. Pause, look, and jump again—that is *three* sights. And then you are landed in the country of the Applepivi!'

"'But how can I jump as far as I can see?'

"'Nothing simpler. Just watch me, and you will be able to do it. I will jump across to the country of the Applepivi and back again in the winking of an eye.'

"So said, so done! With one jump, he leaped to the horizon; the second carried him out of sight; and before I had time to cry out, there he was again standing beside me. I then shook hands with him, thanked him for his jumping lesson, took off with a mighty spring—once, twice, thrice, and found myself safely landed on the snow-white shores of the country of the Applepivi!

"Yes—those three springs landed me sound in wind and limb on the snow-white shores of the country of the Applepivi, into which, before me, no traveller had ever gone. At first I could see no people there, but, in fact, the Applepivi had received warning of the coming of a powerful over-sea leaper, and had retreated to their houses, leaving the open country deserted. But I found a beautiful tree near the sea-shore, on the fruit of which I supped deliciously.

"This fruit was large and oval in shape, the colour of it being a delicate brown, light as puff-paste. On breaking through the crust I found the inside to be luscious, sweet and juicy. The fruit grew in clusters of four at the end of each branch, and some trees were so heavily laden with it as to be almost bent to the ground.

"After I had eaten of this luscious fruit," Tuflongbo went on, "a drowsiness overcame me, and lying down under the tree from whose branches I had plucked it, I enjoyed a long refreshing sleep. I slept till morning, and then rose, wondering where I was. Near me grew a tall plant, like a foxglove, with purple bells, and I picked one long stem. Carrying it, I took my way through mazy groves of fruit-trees, and at last I came suddenly, in an opening, upon a cluster of round straw huts. Out of them poured swarms upon swarms of small people—the Applepivi, humming and buzzing angrily. I turned to fly for my life, and then thought better of it, and drew softly near them, holding out the stem with purple blossoms. After a moment of hesitation, one of the Applepivi darted upon the stem and thrust a round little brown head into the cup of a flower; after which others followed.

"Then I saw that this curious small folk had tiny wings under their shoulders, and talked with a humming noise. The strange thing was, I understood what they said. They first of all asked me my name. 'Tuflungbo,' I answered, and I told them I came from a country across the sea called Shineland.

'Tuflongbo, Tuflongbo!
Back to Shineland let him go!'

some of them buzzed in my ears. But one of them, who had been buried in a purple bell, came out of it, and said, 'Let us hear a little more about it, Tuflongbo. What have you Shineland folk got to give the Applepivi?'

"'We can give you moors of purple heather, and fields of bean-blossom,' I said.

"But the rest of the Applepivi only buzzed the louder:

'Tuflongbo, Tuflongbo!
Back to Shineland let him go!'

"So back I came, over the sea of the three leaps,

and over the wall of the World's End," said Tuflongbo, "and here I am."

"Is that all?" said Muffin. "I don't think much of that. As for your Applepivi, that's only another name for——!"

"Shut up, Muffin!" cried the Fairy Queen. "It's supper-time, and I should like some bread and honey, and apple-pie and cream!"

So they had a jolly good supper, and when it was done, the Fairy Queen told Tuflongbo to stand on his head.

When the Fairy Queen took her last spoonful of apple-pie and cream, an apple-pip that had, by the cook's mistake, got into the pie, made her cough.

"Slap her on the back, Muffin!" said Tuflongbo.

That made her Majesty monstrous angry, and she said, as she took the pip out of her mouth between her finger and thumb:

"I don't think your journey did you any good, Tuflongbo. How much of what you told us is true?"

"Not a word of it, your Majesty," said Tuflongbo, with a grin: "I made it all up as I was eating a Ribston pippin after breakfast."

LAZY JACK

A STORY WITHOUT A MORAL

ONCE upon a time there was a boy whose name was Jack, and he lived with his mother on a dreary common. They were very poor, and the old woman got her living by spinning, but Jack was so lazy that he would do nothing but bask in the sun in the hot weather, and sit by the corner of the hearth in the winter-time. His mother could not get him to do anything for her, and was obliged at last to tell him that if he did not begin to work for his porridge she would turn him out to get his living as he could.

This threat at length roused Jack, and he went out and hired himself for the day to a neighbouring farmer for a penny; but as he was coming home, never having had any money of his own before, he lost it in passing over a brook.

"You stupid boy," said his mother, "you should have put it in your pocket."

"I'll do so another time," replied Jack.

The next day Jack went out again and hired himself to a cowkeeper, who gave him a jar of milk for his day's work. Jack took the jar and put it into the large pocket of his jacket, spilling it all long before he got home.

"Dear me!" said the old woman; "you should have carried it on your head."

"I'll do so another time," said Jack.

The following day Jack hired himself again to a farmer, who agreed to give him a cream cheese for his services. In the evening Jack took the cheese, and went home with it on his head. By the time he got home the cheese was completely spoilt, part of it being lost, and part matted with his hair.

"You stupid lout," said his mother, "you should have carried it very carefully in your hands."

"I'll do so another time," replied Jack.

The day after this Jack again went out, and hired himself to a baker, who would give him nothing for his work but a large tom-cat. Jack took the cat, and began carrying it very carefully in his hands, but in a short time pussy scratched him so much that he was compelled to let it go.

When he got home, his mother said to him: "You silly fellow, you should have tied it with a string, and dragged it along after you."

"I'll do so another time," said Jack.

The next day Jack hired himself to a butcher, who rewarded his labours by the handsome present of a shoulder of mutton. Jack took the mutton, tied it to a string, and trailed it along after him in the dirt, so that by the time he had got home the meat was completely spoilt. His mother was this time quite out of patience with him, for the next day was Sunday, and she was obliged to content herself with cabbage for her dinner.

"You ninny-hammer," said she to her son, "you should have carried it on your shoulder."

"I'll do so another time," replied Jack.

On the Monday Jack went once more, and hired himself to a cattle-keeper, who gave him a donkey for his trouble. Although Jack was very strong, he found some difficulty in hoisting the donkey on his shoulders, but at last he accomplished it, and began walking slowly home with his prize. Now it happened that in the course of his journey there lived a rich man with his only daughter, a beautiful girl, but unfortunately, deaf and dumb; she had never laughed in her life, and the doctors said she would never recover till somebody made her laugh. This young lady happened to be looking out of the window when Jack was passing with the donkey on his shoulders, the legs sticking up in the air, and the sight was so comical that she burst out into a great fit of laughter, and at once recovered her speech and hearing. Her father was overjoyed, and fulfilled his promise by marrying her to Jack, who was thus made a fine gentleman. They lived in a large house, and Jack's mother lived with them in great happiness until she died.

NONSENSE RHYMES

from "Mother Goose's Melody,"
and other great works

A DIRGE

Little Betty Winckle she had a pig,
It was a little pig not very big;
When he was alive he liv'd in clover,
But now he's dead and that's all over;
Johnny Winckle he
Sat down and cry'd,
Betty Winckle she
Laid down and dy'd;
So there was an end of one, two, and three,
Johnny Winckle he,
Betty Winckle she,
And Piggy Wiggie.

A dirge is a song made for the dead; but whether this was made for Betty Winckle or her pig, is uncertain; no notice being taken of it by Camden, or any of the famous antiquarians.—Wall's *System of Sense.*

A MELANCHOLY SONG

Trip upon Trenchers,
And dance upon Dishes,
My Mother sent me for some Bawm, some Bawm:
She bid me tread lightly,
And come again quickly,
For fear the young Men should do me some Harm.
Yet didn't you see,
Yet didn't you see,

What naughty Tricks they put upon me;
They broke my Pitcher,
And spilt the Water,
And hufft my Mother,
And chid her Daughter,
And kiss'd my Sister instead of me.

What a succession of misfortunes befell this poor girl! But the last circumstance was the most affecting, and might have proved fatal.—Winslow's *View of Bath*.

CROSS PATCH

Cross patch, draw the latch,
Set by the fire and spin;
Take a cup and drink it up,
Then call your neighbours in.

A common case this, to call in our neighbours to rejoice when all the good liquor is gone.—Pliny.

AMPHION'S SONG OF EURYDICE

I won't be my father's Jack,
I won't be my father's Gill,
I will be the fiddler's wife,
And have music when I will.
T'other little tune,
T'other little tune,
Prithee, Love, play me
T'other little tune.

Maxim

Those arts are the most valuable which are of the greatest use.

THREE WISE MEN OF GOTHAM

THREE wise men of Gotham,
They went to sea in a bowl,
And if the bowl had been stronger,
My song had been longer.

It is long enough. Never lament the loss of what is not worth having.—BOYLE.

THERE WAS AN OLD MAN

THERE was an old man,
And he had a calf,
And that's half;
He took him out of the stall,
And put him on the wall,
And that's all.

Maxim

Those who are given to tell all they know, generally tell more than they know.

THERE WAS AN OLD WOMAN

THERE was an old woman
Liv'd under a hill,
She put a mouse in a bag,
And sent it to mill:

The miller did swear
By the point of his knife,
He never took toll
Of a mouse in his life.

The only instance of a miller refusing toll, and for which the cat has just cause of complaint against him.

Coke upon Littleton.

DAME UNDER-THE-HILL

THERE was an old woman
Liv'd under a hill,
And if she isn't gone
She lives there still.

This is a self-evident proposition, which is the very essence of truth. "She lived under the hill, and if she is not gone she lives there still." Nobody will presume to contradict this.—CRÆUSA.

PLATO'S SONG

DING dong bell,
The cat is in the well.
Who put her in?
Little Johnny Green.
What a naughty boy was that,
To drown poor Pussy cat,
Who never did any harm,
And kill'd the mice in his father's barn.

Maxim

He that injures one threatens an hundred.

LITTLE TOM TUCKER

LITTLE Tom Tucker
Sings for his supper;
What shall he eat?
White bread and butter:
How will he cut it,
Without e'er a knife?
How will he be married,
Without e'er a wife?

To be married without a wife is a terrible thing, and to be married with a bad wife is something worse; however, a good wife that sings well is the best musical instrument in the world.—PUFFENDORFF.

SEE-SAW, MARGERY DAW,

SEE-SAW, Margery Daw,
Jacky shall have a new master;
Jacky must have but a penny a day,
Because he can work no faster.

It is a mean and scandalous practice in authors to put notes to things that deserve no notice.—GROTIUS.

GREAT A, LITTLE A

GREAT A, little a,
Bouncing B;
The cat's in the cupboard,
And she can't see.

Yes, she can see that you are naughty, and don't mind your book.

SEE-SAW SACARADOWN

SEE-SAW, sacaradown,
Which is the way to London town?
One foot up, the other foot down,
That is the way to London town.

Or to any other town upon the face of the earth.

WICKLIFFE.

SHOE THE COLT

SHOE the colt,
Shoe the colt,
Shoe the wild mare;
Here a nail,
There a nail,
Yet she goes bare.

Ay, ay, drive the nail that will go: that's the way of the world, and is the method pursued by all our financiers, politicians, and necromancers.—VATTEL.

JOHN SMITH

Is John Smith within?
Yes, that he is.
Can he set a shoe?
Aye marry, two.
Here a nail and there a nail,
Tick, tack, too.

Maxim

Knowledge is a treasure, but practice is the key to it.

HIGH DIDDLE DIDDLE

High diddle diddle,
The cat and the fiddle,
  The cow jump'd over the moon;
The little dog laugh'd
To see such craft,
  And the dish ran away with the spoon.

It must be a little dog that laughed, for a great dog would be ashamed to laugh at such nonsense.

RIDE A COCK HORSE

Ride a cock horse
To Banbury Cross,
  To see what Tommy can buy;
A penny white loaf,
A penny white cake,
  And a twopenny apple-pie.

There's a good boy, eat up your pie and hold your tongue; for silence is the sign of wisdom.

COCK A DOODLE DOO

Cock a doodle doo,
My dame has lost her shoe;
My master has lost his fiddle-stick,
And knows not what to do.

The cock crows us up early in the morning, that we may work for our bread, and not live upon charity or upon trust: "for he who lives upon charity shall be often affronted, and he that lives upon trust shall pay double."

THE GROAT

There was an old man
  In a velvet coat,
He kiss'd a maid
  And gave her a groat;
The groat it was crack'd,
And would not go,
Ah, old man, do you serve me so?

Maxim

If the coat be ever so fine that a fool wears, it is still but fool's coat.

ROUND ABOUT, ROUND ABOUT

Round about, round about,
  Maggoty pie;
My Father loves good ale,
  And so do I.

Maxim

Evil company makes the good bad, and the bad worse.

JACK AND GILL

Jack and Gill
Went up the hill,
  To fetch a pail of water;
Jack fell down
And broke his crown,
  And Gill came tumbling after.

Maxim

The more you think of dying, the better you will live.

ARISTOTLE'S STORY

There were two birds sat on a stone,
Fa, la, la, la, lal, de;
One flew away, and then there was one,
Fa, la, la, la, lal, de;
The other flew after,
And then there was none,
Fa, la, la, la, lal, de;
And so the poor stone
Was left all alone,
Fa, la, la, la, lal, de.

This may serve as a chapter of consequence in the next new book of logic.—Sawmill's *Reports*.

HUSH-A-BY BABY

Hush-a-by baby
On the tree top,
When the wind blows
The cradle will rock;
When the bough breaks
The cradle will fall,
Down tumbles baby,
Cradle and all.

This may serve as a warning to the proud and ambitious, who climb so high that they generally fall at last.

Maxim

Content turns all it touches into gold.

LITTLE JACK HORNER

Little Jack Horner
Sat in a corner,
   Eating of Christmas pie;
He put in his thumb,
And pull'd out a plum,
   And what a good boy was I.

Jack was a boy of excellent taste, as should appear by his pulling out a plum; it is therefore supposed that his father apprenticed him to a mince-pie maker, that he might improve his taste from year to year; no one standing in so much need of good taste as a pastrycook.

Bentley, *On the Sublime and Beautiful.*

PEASE-PORRIDGE HOT

Pease-porridge hot,
   Pease-porridge cold,
Pease-porridge in the pot
   Nine days old,
Spell me that in four letters;
   I will, That.

Maxim

The poor are seldomer sick for want of food, than the rich are by the excess of it.

WHO COMES HERE?

WHO comes here?
A grenadier.
What do you want?
A pot of beer.
Where is your money?
I've forgot.
Get you gone,
You drunken sot.

Maxim

Intemperance is attended with diseases, and idleness with poverty.

JACK SPRAT

JACK SPRAT
Could eat no fat,
His wife could eat no lean;
And so betwixt them both
They lick'd the platter clean.

Maxim

Better to go to bed supperless, than rise in debt.

THE BOUNCING GIRL

WHAT care I how black I be,
Twenty pounds will marry me;
If twenty won't, forty shall,
I am my mother's bouncing girl.

Maxim.

If we do not flatter ourselves, the flattery of others would have no effect.

TELL-TALE TIT

TELL-TALE tit,
Your tongue shall be slit,
And all the dogs in our town
Shall have a bit.

Maxim

Point not at the faults of others with a foul finger.

THE HARE

ONE, two, three,
Four and five,
I caught a hare alive;
Six, seven, eight,
Nine and ten,
I let him go again.

Maxim

We may be as good as we please, if we please to be good.

A DOLEFUL DITTY

I

THREE children sliding on the ice
Upon a summer's day,
As it fell out they all fell in,
The rest they ran away.

II

Oh! had these children been at school,
  Or sliding on dry ground,
Ten thousand pounds to one penny
  They had not then been drown'd.

III

Ye parents who have children dear,
  And eke ye that have none,
If you would keep them safe abroad,
  Pray keep them safe at home.

There is something so melancholy in this song, that it has occasioned many people to shed tears. It is almost as tearful as the tune which John the coachman whistles to his horses.—TRUMPINGTON'S *Travels.*

PATTY CAKE

PATTY cake, patty cake,
  Baker's man;
That I will master
  As fast as I can;
Prick it, and prick it,
  And mark it with a T,
And there will be enough
  For Jacky and me.

Maxim

The surest way to gain our ends is to moderate our desires.

WHEN I WAS A LITTLE BOY

WHEN I was a little boy
  I had but little wit,
'Tis a long time ago,
  And I have no more yet;
Nor ever, ever shall,
  Until that I die,
For the longer I live,
  The more fool am I.

Maxim

He that will be his own master has often a fool for his scholar.

THE WHEEL-BARROW

I

WHEN I was a little boy
  I liv'd by myself,
And all the bread
And cheese I got
  I laid upon the shelf;
The rats and the mice
  They made such a strife,
That I was forc'd to go to town
  And buy me a wife.

II

The streets were so broad,
  The lanes were so narrow,
I was forc'd to bring my wife home
  In a wheel-barrow;

The wheel-barrow broke,
And my wife had a fall.
Farewell
Wheel-barrow, wife and all.

Maxim

Provide against the worst, and hope for the best.

O MY KITTEN A KITTEN

O MY kitten a kitten,
And oh! my kitten, my deary,
Such a sweet pap as this
There is not far nor neary;
There we go up, up, up,
Here we go down, down, down,
Here we go backwards and forwards,
And here we go round, round, round.

Maxim

Idleness hath no advocate, but many friends.

THIS PIG WENT TO MARKET

THIS pig went to market,
That pig stayed at home;
This pig had roast meat,
That pig had none;
This pig went to the barn-door,
And cried week, week, for more.

Maxim

If we do not govern our passions, our passions will govern us.

ALEXANDER'S SONG

THERE was a man of Thessaly,
And he was wondrous wise,
He jump'd into a quick-set hedge,
And scratch'd out both his eyes:
And when he saw his eyes were out,
With all his might and main
He jump'd into another hedge,
And scratch'd them in again.

How happy it was for the man to scratch his eyes in again, when they were scratched out! But he was a blockhead or he would have kept himself out of the hedge, and not been scratched at all.

WISEMAN'S *New Way to Wisdom.*

A PIG

A LONG-TAIL'D pig, or a short-tail'd pig,
Or a pig without any tail;
A sow pig, or a boar pig,
Or a pig with a curling tail.

Take hold of the tail and eat off his head,
And then you'll be sure the pig-hog is dead.

CÆSAR'S SONG

Bow, wow, wow,
Whose dog art thou?
Little Tom Tinker's dog,
Bow, wow, wow.

Tom Tinker's dog is a very good dog, and an honester dog than his master.

BAH, BAH, BLACK SHEEP

Bah, bah, black sheep,
  Have you any wool?
Yes, marry have I,
  Three bags full;
One for my master,
  One for my dame,
But none for the little boy
  Who cries in the lane.

Maxim

Bad habits are easier conquered to-day than to-morrow.

ROBIN AND RICHARD

Robin and Richard
  Were two pretty men,
They lay in bed
  'Till the clock struck ten:
Then up starts Robin
  And looks at the sky,
Oh! brother Richard,
  The sun's very high;
You go before
  With the bottle and bag,
And I will come after
  On little Jack nag.

What lazy rogues are these to lie in bed so long! I dare say they have no clothes to their backs; for "laziness clothes a man with rags."

HOT PIES AND COLD PIES

THERE was an old woman,
  And she sold puddings and pies,
She went to the mill
  And the dust flew into her eyes:
Hot pies,
  And cold pies to sell,
Wherever she goes
  You may follow her by the smell.

Maxim

Either say nothing of the absent, or speak like a friend.

JACK AND GILL

THERE were two blackbirds
  Sat upon a hill,
The one was nam'd Jack,
  The other nam'd Gill;
Fly away, Jack,
  Fly away, Gill,
Come again, Jack,
  Come again, Gill.

Maxim

A bird in the hand is worth two in the bush.

THE SOW CAME IN WITH A SADDLE

THE sow came in with a saddle,
The little pig rock'd the cradle,
The dish jump'd a-top of the table,
To see the pot wash the ladle;
The spit that stood behind the wall
Call'd the dishclout dirty troll;
"Ods-plut!" says the gridiron,
"Can't ye agree!
I'm the head constable,
Bring 'em to me."

Note

If he acts as constable in this case, the cook must surely be the justice of peace.

BOYS AND GIRLS COME OUT TO PLAY

BOYS and girls come out to play,
The moon does shine as bright as day;
Come with a hoop, and come with a call,
Come with a good will or not at all.
Lose your supper, and lose your sleep,
Come to your playfellows in the street;
Up the ladder and down the wall;
A halfpenny loaf will serve us all.

But when the loaf is gone, what will you do?
Those who would eat must work.

Maxim

All work and no play makes Jack a dull boy.

DAUGHTER JANE

We're three brethren out of Spain
Come to court your daughter Jane:
My daughter Jane she is too young,
She has no skill in a flattering tongue.
Be she young, or be she old,
It's for her gold she must be sold;
So fare you well, my lady gay,
We must return another day.

Maxim

Riches serve a wise man, and govern a fool.

A LOGICAL SONG, OR THE CONJURER'S REASON FOR NOT GETTING MONEY

I would, if I cou'd,
If I cou'dn't, how cou'd I?
I cou'dn't, without I cou'd, cou'd I?
Cou'd you, without you cou'd, cou'd ye?
    Cou'd ye, Cou'd ye?
Cou'd you, without you cou'd, cou'd ye?

Note

This is a new way of handling an old argument, said to be invented by a famous senator; but it has something in it of Gothic construction.—Sanderson.

A LEARNED SONG

HERE'S A, B, and C,
D, E, F, and G,
H, I, K, L, M, N, O, P, Q,
  R, S, T, and U,
W, X, Y, and Z.
And here's the child's dad,
Who is sagacious and discerning,
And knows this is the fount of learning.

Note

This is the most learned ditty in the world: for indeed there is no song can be made without the aid of this, it being the gamut and groundwork of them all.

MOPE'S *Geography of the Mind.*

A SEASONABLE SONG

PIPING hot, smoking hot,
What I've got,
You have not,
Hot grey pease, hot, hot, hot;
Hot grey pease hot.

There is more music in this song, on a cold frosty night, than ever the Sirens were possessed of, who captivated Ulysses; and the effects stick closer to the ribs.

HUGGLEFORD, *On Hunger.*

DICKERY, DICKERY, DOCK

Dickery, dickery, dock,
The mouse ran up the clock;
The clock struck one,
The mouse ran down,
Dickery, dickery dock.

Maxim

Time stays for no man.

FAREWELL TO THE FAIRIES

Farewell rewards and fairies,
Good housewives now may say,
For now foul sluts in dairies
Do fare as well as they.
And though they sweep their hearths no less
Than maids were wont to do,
Yet who of late, for cleanliness,
Finds sixpence in her shoe?

Lament, lament, old Abbeys,
The fairies' lost command;
They did but change priests' babies,
But some have changed your land;
And all your children sprung from thence
Are now grown Puritans;
Who live as changelings ever since,
For love of your domains.

At morning and at evening both,
  You merry were and glad,
So little care of sleep or sloth
  These pretty ladies had;
When Tom came home from labour,
  Or Cis to milking rose,
Then merrily went their tabor,
  And nimbly went their toes.

Witness those rings and roundelays
  Of theirs, which yet remain,
Were footed in Queen Mary's days
  On many a grassy plain;
But since of late Elizabeth,
  And later, James came in,
They never danced on any heath
  As when the time hath been.

By which we note the fairies
  Were of the old profession,
Their songs were Ave-Maries,
  Their dances were procession:
But now, alas! they all are dead,
  Or gone beyond the seas;
Or farther for religion fled,
  Or else they take their ease.

A tell-tale in their company
  They never could endure,
And whoso kept not secretly
  Their mirth, was punished sure;
It was a just and Christian deed,
  To pinch such black and blue:
O how the commonwealth doth need
  Such justices as you!

ELEGY ON THE DEATH OF A MAD DOG

Good people all, of every sort,
  Give ear unto my song:
And if you find it wond'rous short,
  It cannot hold you long.

In Islington there was a man,
  Of whom the world might say,
That still a godly race he ran,
  Whene'er he went to pray.

A kind and gentle heart he had,
  To comfort friends and foes;
The naked every day he clad,
  When he put on his clothes.

And in that town a dog was found,
  As many dogs there be,
Both mongrel, puppy, whelp, and hound,
  And curs of low degree.

This dog and man at first were friends;
  But when a pique began,
The dog, to gain some private ends,
  Went mad and bit the man.

Around from all the neighbouring streets
  The wond'ring neighbours ran,
And swore the dog had lost his wits,
  To bite so good a man.

The wound it seem'd both sore and sad
  To every Christian eye;
And while they swore the dog was mad,
  They swore the man would die.

But soon a wonder came to light,
  That show'd the rogues they lied:
The man recover'd of the bite,
  The dog it was that died.

PIGWIGGEN

PIGWIGGEN arms him for the field,
A little cockle-shell his shield,
Which he could very bravely wield,
  Yet could it not be pierced;
His spear a bent both stiff and strong,
And well near of two inches long:
The pile was of a horse-fly's tongue,
  Whose sharpness naught reversed.

And puts him on a coat of mail,
Which was of a fish's scale,
That, when his foe should him assail,
  No point should be prevailing:
His rapier was a hornet's sting;
It was a very dangerous thing,
For if he chanc'd to hurt the king,
  It would be long in healing.

His helmet was a beetle's head,
Most horrible and full of dread,
That able was to strike one dead,
  Yet it did well become him:

And, for a plume, a horse's hair,
Which, being tossed with the air,
Had force to strike his foe with fear
  And turn his weapon from him.

Himself he on an earwig set,
Yet scarce he on his back could get,
So oft and high he did curvet,
  Ere he himself could settle:
He made him turn, and stop, and bound,
To gallop, and to trot the round,
He scarce could stand on any ground,
  He was so full of mettle.

When soon he met with Tomalin,
One that a valiant knight had been,
And to great Oberon of kin:
  Quoth he, "Thou manly fairy,
Tell Oberon I come prepar'd,
Then bid him stand upon his guard;
This hand his baseness shall reward,
  Let him be ne'er so wary.

"Say to him thus, that I defy
His slanders and his infamy,
And as a mortal enemy
  Do publicly proclaim him:
Withal, that if I had mine own,
He should not wear the fairy crown,
But with a vengeance should come down;
  Nor we a king should name him!"

THE OLD MAN OF THE SEA

A NIGHTMARE DREAM BY DAYLIGHT

Do you know the Old Man of the Sea, of the Sea?
Have you met with that dreadful old man?
If you haven't been caught, you will be, you will be;
For catch you he must and he can.

He doesn't hold on by your throat, by your throat,
As of old in the terrible tale;
But he grapples you tight by the coat, by the coat,
Till its buttons and button-holes fail.

There's the charm of a snake in his eye, in his eye,
And a polypus-grip in his hands;
You cannot go back, nor get by, nor get by,
If you look at the spot where he stands.

Oh, you're grabbed! See his claw on your sleeve, on your sleeve!
It is Sinbad's Old Man of the Sea!
You're a Christian, no doubt you believe, you believe:
You're a martyr, whatever you be!

—Is the breakfast-hour past? They must wait, they must wait,
While the coffee boils sullenly down,
While the Johnny-cake burns on the grate, on the grate,
And the toast is done frightfully brown.

—Yes, your dinner will keep; let it cool, let it cool,
And Madam may worry and fret,
And children half-starved go to school, go to school;
He can't think of sparing you yet.

—Hark! the bell for the train! "Come along! Come along!
For there isn't a second to lose."
"ALL ABOARD!" (He holds on.) "Fsht! ding-dong! Fsht! ding-dong!"—
You can follow on foot, if you choose.

—There's a maid with a cheek like a peach, like a peach,
That is waiting for you in the church;—
But he clings to your side like a leech, like a leech,
And you leave your lost bride in the lurch.

—There's a babe in a fit,—hurry quick! hurry quick!
To the doctor's as fast as you can!
The baby is off, while you stick, while you stick
In the grip of the dreadful Old Man!

—I have looked on the face of the Bore, of the Bore;
The voice of the Simple I know;
I have welcomed the Flat at my door, at my door;
I have sat by the side of the Slow;

I have walked like a lamb by the Friend, by the Friend,
That stuck to my skirts like a bur;
I have borne the stale talk without end, without end,
Of the sitter whom nothing could stir:

But my hamstrings grow loose, and I shake, and I
shake,
At the sight of the dreadful Old Man;
Yea, I quiver and quake, and I take, and I take
To my legs with what vigour I can!

Oh, the dreadful Old Man of the Sea, of the Sea!
He's come back like the Wandering Jew!
He has had his cold claw upon me, upon me,—
And be sure that he'll have it on you!

THE BALLAD OF THE OYSTERMAN

It was a tall young oysterman lived by the river-side,
His shop was just upon the bank, his boat was on
the tide;
The daughter of a fisherman, that was so straight
and slim,
Lived over on the other bank, right opposite to him.

It was the pensive oysterman that saw a lovely
maid,
Upon a moonlight evening, a-sitting in the shade;
He saw her wave her handkerchief, as much as if to
say,
"I'm wide awake, young oysterman, and all the
folks away."

Then up arose the oysterman, and to himself said he,
"I guess I'll leave the skiff at home, for fear that
folks should see;
I read it in the story-book, that, for to kiss his dear,
Leander swam the Hellespont,—and I will swim
this here."

And he has leaped into the waves, and crossed the shining stream,
And he has clambered up the bank, all in the moonlight gleam;
Oh, there were kisses sweet as dew, and words as soft as rain,—
But they have heard her father's step, and in he leaps again!

Out spoke the ancient fisherman: "Oh, what was that, my daughter?"
"'Twas nothing but a pebble, sir, I threw into the water."
"And what is that, pray tell me, love, that paddles off so fast?"
"It's nothing but a porpoise, sir, that's been a-swimming past."

Out spoke the ancient fisherman: "Now, bring me my harpoon!
I'll get into my fishing-boat, and fix the fellow soon."
Down fell the pretty innocent, as falls a snow-white lamb;
Her hair drooped round her pallid cheeks, like seaweed on a clam.

Alas for those two loving ones! she waked not from her swound,
And he was taken with a cramp, and in the waves was drowned;
But Fate has metamorphosed them, in pity of their woe,
And now they keep an oyster-shop for mermaids down below.

NURSERY NONSENSE

THERE LIVED AN OLD MAN

There lived an old man in a garret,
So afraid of a little tom-cat,
That he pulled himself up to the ceiling,
And hung himself up in his hat.

And for fear of the wind and the rain
He took his umbrella to bed—
I've half an idea that silly old man
Was a little bit wrong in his head.

CRAZY ARITHMETIC

4 in 2 goes twice as fast,
  If 2 and 4 change places:
But how can 2 and 3 make four,
  If 3 and 2 make faces?

ONCE UPON A TIME

ONCE upon a time, in a little wee house,
  Lived a funny old Man and his Wife;
And he said something funny to make her laugh
  Every day of his life.

One day he said a very funny thing,
  That she shook and screamed with laughter;
But the poor old soul, she couldn't leave off
  For at least three whole days after.

THREE POOR BEGGAR-MEN

THREE poor Beggar-men came to town,
And they begg'd all day from door to door;
But they didn't get a bite from morn to night,
So they said they would beg no more, no more.

Now, when first they came, they were blind and lame,
And they walk'd on wooden legs all that day;
But the rogues could see, as well as you or me,
When they *ran* away, away, away!

COCK-A-DOODLE-DOO

A LITTLE boy got out of bed,
'Twas only six o'clock;
And out of window poked his head,
And spied a crowing Cock.

The little boy said, "Mr. Bird,
Pray tell me, who are you?"
And all the answer that he heard
Was "Cock-a-doodle-doo."

OLD WEATHERWITCH

"Blow, Wind, Blow,"
  Three sailors sang together:
But "Nay, nay, nay," they heard her say,
  The old Witch of the weather.

So in their tiny boat
  They sat, those sailors three;
Till the wind should blow, they couldna go
  A-sailing on the sea.

COCK SPARROW

An inquisitive Cock Sparrow
  Ask'd every man in Wales,
Why Parrots had long noses,
  And Foxes had long tails.

Some said, that Foxes used their tails
  In winter for a muff;
And Parrots' noses all were long,
  Because they all took snuff.

But the reason, so it seems to me,
  As perhaps it will to you,
Is that they once tried short tails,
  And short tails wouldn't do.

SIR BUNNY

Sir Bunny is a splendid shot,
And every time he fires,
A farmer or a keeper falls,
Sometimes a brace of squires.

He went out shooting yesterday
With young Lord Leveret;
But the wind it blew, and the rain it pour'd,
And both got soaking wet.

FOUR ODDMENTS AND AN ODDITY

TEN LITTLE INJUNS

Ten little Injuns standin' in a line,
One toddled home and then there were nine;
Nine little Injuns swingin' on a gate,
One tumbled off and then there were eight.

> One little, two little, three little, four little, five little Injun boys,
> Six little, seven little, eight little, nine little, ten little Injun boys.

Eight little Injuns gayest under heav'n,
One went to sleep and then there were seven;
Seven little Injuns cutting up their tricks,
One broke his neck and then there were six.

Six little Injuns kickin' all alive,
One kick'd the bucket and then there were five;
Five little Injuns on a cellar door,
One tumbled in and then there were four.

Four little Injuns up on a spree,
One he got fuddled and then there were three;
Three little Injuns out in a canoe,
One tumbled overboard and then there were two.

Two little Injuns foolin' with a gun,
One shot t'other and then there was one;
One little Injun livin' all alone,
He got married and then there were none.

BOBBY BINGO

THE miller's dog lay at the door,
And his name was Bobby Bingo:
B with an I, I with an N, N with a G, G with an O,
His name was Bobby Bingo.

The miller he bought a barrel of ale,
And he called it right good Stingo:
S with a T, T with an I, I with an N, N with a G,
G with an O,
He called it right good Stingo.

The miller he went to town one day,
And he bought a wedding ring-o:
R with an I, I with an N, N with a G, G with an O,
He bought a wedding ring-o.

The miller, he took it home to his dog,
And his dog was Bobby Bingo:
B with an I, I with an N, N with a G, G with an O,
His name was Bobby Bingo.

TOM OF THE GOATSKIN

Long ago, a poor widow woman lived down near the iron forge, by Enniscorthy, and she was so poor, she had no clothes to put on her son; so she used to fix him in the ash-hole, near the fire, and pile the warm ashes about him; and according as he grew up, she sunk the pit deeper. At last, by hook or by crook, she got a goatskin, and fastened it round his waist, and he felt quite grand, and took a walk down the street. So says she to him next morning, "Tom, you thief, you never done any good yet, and you six foot high, and past nineteen; take that rope, and bring me a faggot from the wood." "Never say't twice, mother," says Tom—"here goes."

When he had it gathered and tied, what should come up but a big *joiant*, nine foot high, and made a lick of a club at him. Well become Tom, he jumped a-one side, and picked up a ram-pike; and the first crack he gave the big fellow, he made him kiss the clod. "If you have e'er a prayer," says Tom, "now's the time to say it, before I make small scraps of you." "I have no prayers," says the giant; "but if you spare my life I'll give you that club; and as long as you keep from sin, you'll win every battle you ever fight with it."

Tom made no bones about letting him off; and as soon as he got the club in his hands, he sat down on the faggot and gave it a tap, and says, "Bresna,

I had a great trouble gathering you, and run the risk of my life for you; the least you can do is to carry me home." And sure enough, the wind o' the word was all it wanted. It went off through the wood, groaning and cracking, till it came to the widow's door.

Well, when the sticks were all burned, Tom was sent off again to pick more; and this time he had to fight with a giant that had two heads on him. Tom had a little more trouble with him—that's all; and the prayers *he* said, was to give Tom a fife, that nobody could help dancing when he was playing it. And then he made the big faggot dance home, with himself sitting on it. The next giant was a beautiful boy with three heads on him. He had neither prayers nor catechism no more *nor* the others; and so he gave Tom a bottle of green ointment, that wouldn't let you be burned, nor scalded, nor wounded. "And now," says he, "there's no more of us. You may come and gather sticks here till harvest, without giant or fairy-man to disturb you."

Well, now, Tom was prouder nor ten paycocks, and used to take a walk down street in the heel of the evening; but some o' the little boys had no manners, and put out their tongues at Tom's club and Tom's goatskin. He didn't like that at all, and it would be mean to give one of them a clout. At last, what should come through the town but a kind of a bellman, only it's a big bugle he had, and a huntsman's cap on his head, and a kind of a painted shirt. So this—he wasn't a bellman, and I don't know what to call him—bugle-man, maybe, proclaimed that the King of Dublin's daughter was so melancholy that she didn't give a laugh for seven years, and that her father would grant her in marriage to whoever could make her laugh three times. "That's the very thing for me to try," says Tom; and so, without burning any more daylight, he kissed his mother, curled his club at the little boys, and off he set along the yalla highroad to the town of Dublin.

At last Tom came to one of the city gates, and the guards laughed at him instead of letting him in. Tom stood it all for a little time, but at last one of them—out of fun, as he said—drove his bayonet half an inch or so into his side. Tom done nothing but take the fellow by the scruff o' the neck and the waistband of his corduroys, and fling him into the canal. Some run to pull the fellow out, and others to let manners into the vulgarian with their swords and daggers; but a tap from his club sent them headlong into the moat or down on the stones, and they were soon begging him to stay his hands.

So at last one of them was glad enough to show Tom the way to the palace-yard; and there was the king, and the queen, and the princess, in a gallery, looking at all sorts of wrestling, and sword-playing, and long dances, and mumming, all to please the princess; but not a smile came over her handsome face.

Well, they all stopped when they seen the young giant, with his boy's face, and long black hair, and his short, curly beard—for his poor mother couldn't afford to buy razors—and his great strong arms, and bare legs, and no covering but the goatskin that reached from his waist to his knees. But a wizened misery of a fellow, with a red head, that wished to be married to the princess, and didn't like how she opened her eyes at Tom, came forward and asked his business. "My business," says Tom, says he, "is to make the beautiful princess, God bless her, laugh three times." "Do you see all them merry fellows and skilful swordsmen," says the other, "that could eat you up with a grain of salt, and not a mother's soul of 'em ever got a laugh from her these seven years?" So the fellows gathered round Tom, and the bad man aggravated him till he told them he didn't care a pinch o' snuff for the whole bilin' of 'em; let 'em come on, six at a time, and try what they could do. The king, that was too far off to hear what they were saying, asked what did the stranger want. "He wants," says the red-headed fellow, "to make hares of your best men." "Oh!" says the king, "if that's the way, let one of 'em turn out and try his mettle." So one stood forward, with sword and pot-lid, and made a cut at Tom. He struck the fellow's elbow with the club, and up over their heads flew the sword, and down went the owner of it on the gravel from a thump he got on the helmet. Another took his place, and another, and another, and then half-dozen at once, and Tom sent swords, helmets, shields, and bodies rolling over and over, and themselves bawling out that they were kilt, and rubbing their poor elbows and hips, and limping away. Tom contrived not to kill anyone; and the princess was so amused, that she let a great sweet laugh out of her that was heard over all the yard. "King of Dublin," says Tom, "I've a quarter of your daughter." And the king didn't know whether he was glad or sorry, and all the blood in the princess's heart run into her cheeks.

So there was no more fighting that day, and

Tom was invited to dine with the royal family. Next day, Redhead told Tom of a wolf, the size of a yearling heifer, that used to be serenading about the walls, and eating people and cattle; and said what a pleasure it would give the king to have it killed. "With all my heart," says Tom; "send a jackeen to show me where he lives, and we'll see how he behaves to a stranger." The princess was not well pleased, for Tom looked a different person with fine clothes and a nice green cap over his long curly hair; and besides he'd got one laugh out of her. However, the king gave his consent; and in an hour and a half the horrible wolf was walking into the palace-yard, and Tom a step or two behind, with his club on his shoulder, just as a shepherd would be walking after a pet lamb.

The king and queen and princess were safe up in their gallery, but the officers and people of the court that were patrolling about the place, when they saw the big baste coming in, gave themselves up, and began to make for doors and gates; and the wolf licked his chops, as if he was saying, "Wouldn't I enjoy a breakfast off a couple of yez!" The king shouted out, "O Gilla na Chreck, take away that terrible wolf, and you must have all my daughter." But Tom didn't mind him a bit. He pulled out his flute and began to play like vengeance; and dickens a man or boy in the yard but began shovelling away heel and toe, and the wolf himself was obliged to get on his hind legs and dance along with the rest. A good deal of the people got inside and shut the doors, the way the hairy fellow wouldn't pin them; but Tom kept playing, and the outsiders kept dancing and shouting, and the wolf kept dancing and roaring with the pain his legs were giving him: and all the time he had his eyes on Redhead, who was shut out along with the rest. Wherever Redhead went, the wolf followed, and kept one eye on him and the other on Tom, to see if he would give him leave to eat him. But Tom shook his head, and never stopped the tune, and Redhead never stopped dancing and bawling, and the wolf dancing and roaring, one leg up and the other down, and he ready to drop out of his standing from fair tiresomeness.

ROBIN GOODFELLOW

FROM Oberon, in fairy land,
  The king of ghosts and shadows there,
Mad Robin I, at his command,
  Am sent to view the night-sports here.
      What revel rout
      Is kept about,
  In every corner where I go,
      I will o'ersee,
      And merry be,
  And make good sport, with ho, ho, ho!

More swift than lightning can I fly
  About this airy welkin soon,
And in a minute's space, descry
  Each thing that's done below the moon.
    There's not a hag
    Or ghost shall wag,
  Or cry, 'ware goblins! where I go;
    But Robin I
    Their feats will spy,
  And send them home with ho, ho, ho!

Whene'er such wanderers I meet,
  As from their night-sports they trudge home,
With counterfeiting voice I greet,
  And call them on with me to roam:
    Through woods, through lakes;
    Through bogs, through brakes;
  Or else, unseen, with them I go,
    All in the nick,
    To play some trick,
  And frolic it, with ho, ho, ho!

Sometimes I meet them like a man,
  Sometimes an ox, sometimes a hound;
And to a horse I turn me can,
  To trip and trot about them round.
    But if to ride
    My back they stride,
  More swift than wind away I go,
    O'er hedge and lands,
    Through pools and ponds,
  I hurry, laughing, ho, ho, ho!

When lads and lasses merry be,
With possets and with junkets fine;
Unseen of all the company,
I eat their cakes and sip their wine!
And, to make sport,
I puff and snort:
And out the candles I do blow:
The maids I kiss,
They shriek—Who's this?
I answer naught, but ho, ho, ho!

Yet now and then, the maids to please,
At midnight I card up their wool;
And, while they sleep and take their ease,
With wheel to threads their flax I pull.
I grind at mill
Their malt up still;
I dress their hemp; I spin their tow;
If any wake,
And would me take,
I wend me, laughing, ho, ho, ho!

When house or hearth doth sluttish lie,
I pinch the maidens black and blue;
The bed-clothes from the bed pull I,
And lay them naked all to view.
'Twixt sleep and wake,
I do them take,
And on the key-cold floor them throw;
If out they cry,
Then forth I fly,
And loudly laugh out, ho, ho, ho!

When any need to borrow aught,
  We lend them what they do require;
And, for the use, demand we naught;
  Our own is all we do desire.
      If to repay
      They do delay,
  Abroad amongst them then I go,
      And night by night,
      I them affright,
  With pinchings, dreams, and ho, ho, ho!

When lazy queens have naught to do,
  But study how to cog and lie:
To make debate and mischief too,
  'Twixt one another secretly:
      I mark their gloze,
      And it disclose
  To them whom they have wrongèd so:
      When I have done,
      I get me gone,
  And leave them scolding, ho, ho, ho!

When men do traps and engines set
  In loopholes, where the vermin creep,
Who from their folds and houses get
  Their ducks and geese, and lambs and sheep;
      I spy the gin,
      And enter in,
  And seem a vermin taken so;
      But when they there
      Approach me near,
  I leap out laughing, ho, ho, ho!

By wells and rills and meadows green,
We nightly dance our heyday guise;
And to our fairy king and queen
We chant our moonlight minstrelsies.
When larks 'gin sing,
Away we fling;
And babes new-born steal as we go;
And elf in bed
We leave instead,
And wend us laughing, ho, ho, ho!

From hag-bred Merlin's time, have I
Thus nightly revell'd to and fro;
And for my pranks men call me by
The name of Robin Goodfellow.
Fiends, ghosts and sprites,
Who haunt the nights,
The hags and goblins do me know;
And beldames old
My feats have told,
So *Vale*, *vale*; ho, ho, ho!

THE
GREAT
PANJANDRUM
HIMSELF

So she went into the garden
to cut a cabbage-leaf
to make an apple-pie;
and at the same time
a great she-bear, coming down the street,
pops its head into the shop.
What! no soap?
So he died,
and she very imprudently married the Barber:
and there were present
the Picninnies,
and the Joblillies,
and the Garyulies,
and the great Panjandrum himself,
with the little round button at top;
and they all fell to playing the game
of catch-as-catch-can,
till the gunpowder ran out at the heels of their boots.

(BUT WHERE'S HIS TAIL?)

Everyman
A selection of titles

*indicates volumes available in paperback

Complete lists of Everyman's Library and Everyman Paperbacks are available from the Sales Department, J.M. Dent and Sons Ltd, 91 Clapham High Street, London SW4 7TA

BIOGRAPHY

**Autobiography of Richard Baxter*
Bligh, William. *A Book of the 'Bounty'*
*Chesterfield, Lord. *Letters to His Son and Others*
Cibber, Colley. *An Apology for the Life of Colley Cibber*
*Dana, Richard Henry. *Two Years Before the Mast*
*De Quincey, Thomas. *Confessions of an English Opium-Eater*
Forster, John. *Life of Charles Dickens* (2 vols)
*Gaskell, Elizabeth. *The Life of Charlotte Brontë*
*Gilchrist, Alexander. *The Life of William Blake*
*Hudson, W.H. *Far Away and Long Ago*
*Johnson, Samuel. *Lives of the English Poets: a selection*
**Johnson on Johnson*
Pepys, Samuel. *Diary* (3 vols)
Thomas, Dylan
  **Adventures in the Skin Trade*
  **Portrait of the Artist as a Young Dog*
Tolstoy, Leo. *Childhood, Boyhood and Youth*
Vasari, Giorgio. *Lives of the Painters, Sculptors, and Architects* (4 vols)

ESSAYS AND CRITICISM

*Bacon, Francis. *Essays*
*Coleridge, Samuel Taylor. *Biographia Literaria*
*Emerson, Ralph. *Essays*
*Jerome, Jerome K. *Idle Thoughts of an Idle Fellow*

*Milton, John. *Prose Writings*
Montaigne, Michael Eyquem de. *Essays* (3 vols)
Spencer, Herbert. *Essays on Education and Kindred Subjects*
*Swift, Jonathan. *Tale of a Tub and other satires*

FICTION

*Alcott, Louisa May. *Little Women*
**American Short Stories of the Nineteenth Century*
Austen, Jane
  **Emma*
  **Mansfield Park*
  **Northanger Abbey*
  **Persuasion*
  **Pride and Prejudice*
  **Sense and Sensibility*
**Australian Short Stories*
*Barbusse, Henri. *Under Fire*
Bennett, Arnold
  **The Card*
  **The Old Wives' Tale*
Boccaccio, Giovanni. *The Decameron*
Brontë, Anne
  **Agnes Grey*
  **The Tenant of Wildfell Hall*
Brontë, Charlotte
  **Jane Eyre*
  **The Professor* and *Emma* (a fragment)
  **Shirley*
  **Villette*
*Brontë, Emily. *Wuthering Heights* and *Poems*
Bunyan, John
  **Pilgrim's Progress*
  **Grace Abounding* and *Mr Badman*
*Carroll, Lewis. *Alice in Wonderland*
Collins, Wilkie
  **The Moonstone*
  **The Woman in White*
*Conrad, Joseph. *Lord Jim*

Conrad, Joseph
The Nigger of the 'Narcissus', Typhoon, Falk and other stories
**Youth, Heart of Darkness* and *The End of the Tether*
*Crane, Stephen, *The Red Badge of Courage*
*De Queiroz, Eça. *The Maias*
*Defoe, Daniel. *Moll Flanders*
Dickens, Charles
Barnaby Rudge
**A Christmas Carol* and *The Chimes*
**Christmas Stories*
**Hard Times*
**Nicholas Nickleby*
**Oliver Twist*
**The Pickwick Papers*
**A Tale of Two Cities*
Dostoyevsky, Fyodor
**The House of the Dead*
**Poor Folk* and *The Gambler*
Doyle, Arthur Conan
**The Adventures of Sherlock Holmes*
**The Hound of the Baskervilles*
Eliot, George
**Adam Bede*
**Felix Holt the Radical*
**The Mill on the Floss*
**Scenes of Clerical Life*
**Silas Marner*
**Famous Chinese Short Stories*
*Fielding, Henry. *Joseph Andrews* and *Shamela*
Forster, E.M. *A Passage to India*
Gaskell, Elizabeth
**Cranford*
**Ruth*
**Sylvia's Lovers*
**Wives and Daughters*
*Gissing, Oliver. *The Nether World*
*Goldsmith, Oliver. *The Vicar of Wakefield*
*Grossmith, George and Weedon. *Diary of a Nobody*

Hardy, Thomas
  *_Far from the Madding Crowd_
  *_Jude the Obscure_
  *_The Mayor of Casterbridge_
  *_Stories and Poems_
  *_Tess of the d'Urbervilles_
*Hartley, L.P. _The Travelling Grave_
James, Henry
  *_The Golden Bowl_
  *_Portrait of a Lady_
  *_Selected Tales_
  *_The Turn of the Screw_
*Jefferies, Richard. _Bevis: The Story of a Boy_
*Kipling, Rudyard. _Selected Stories_
*Lamb, Charles and Mary. _Tales from Shakespeare_
*Lawrence, D.H. _Short Stories_
*MacDonald, George. _Phantastes_
*Mansfield, Katherine. _Short Stories_
*Maupassant, Guy de. _Short Stories_
*_Modern Short Stories to 1940_
*_Modern Short Stories 2 (1940–1980)_
*Oliphant, Margaret. _Kirsteen_
*Poe, Edgar Allan. _Tales of Mystery and Imagination_
Pushkin, Alexander. _The Captain's Daughter and other stories_
Richardson, Samuel
  Clarissa (4 vols)
  *_Pamela_ (2 vols)
Roth, Joseph
  *_Flight Without End_
  *_Weights and Measures_
*_Russian Short Stories_
*Saki. _Short Stories 1_ and 2
*Sayers, Dorothy L. _Great Tales of Detection_
Scott, Walter
  The Abbott
  *_The Bride of Lammermoor_
  *_Heart of Mid-Lothian_
  Ivanhoe
  *_Redgauntlet_

Scott, Walter
Rob Roy
The Talisman

*Shelley, Mary Wollstonecraft. *Frankenstein*

*Smollett, Tobias. *Roderick Random*

*Somerville and Ross. *Some Experiences of an Irish R.M.* and *Further Experiences of an Irish R.M.*

*Sterne, Lawrence. *Tristram Shandy*

Stevenson, R.L.
Kidnapped
The Master of Ballantrae and *Weir of Hermiston*

*Swift, Jonathan. *Gulliver's Travels*

*Thackeray, W.M. *Vanity Fair*

Thirteen Famous Ghost Stories

*Thomas, Dylan. *The Collected Stories*

*Tolstoy, Leo. *Master and Man and other parables and tales*

Trollope, Anthony
Dr Thorne
Last Chronicle of Barset
The Warden

*Twain, Mark. *Tom Sawyer* and *Huckleberry Finn*

Victorian Short Stories

*Voltaire. *Candide and other tales*

Wells, H.G.
The Time Machine
The Wheels of Chance

*Wilde Oscar. *The Picture of Dorian Gray*

*Wood, Mrs Henry. *East Lynne*

Woolf, Virginia. *To the Lighthouse*

HISTORY

The Anglo-Saxon Chronicle

*Burnet, Gilbert. *History of His Own Time*

Gibbon, Edward. *The Decline and Fall of the Roman Empire* (6 vols)

*Hollingshead, John. *Ragged London in 1861*

*Stow, John. *The Survey of London*

*Woodhouse, A.S.P. *Puritanism and Liberty*

LEGENDS AND SAGAS

**Beowulf and Its Analogues*
*Chrétien de Troyes. *Arthurian Romances*
**Egils saga*
**Kudrun*
**The Mabinogion*
**The Saga of Gisli*
**The Saga of Grettir the Strong*
*Snorri Sturluson. *Edda*
*Wace and Layamon. *Arthurian Chronicles*

POETRY AND DRAMA

**Anglo-Saxon Poetry*
*Arnold, Matthew. *Selected Poems and Prose*
*Blake, William. *Selected Poems*
*Brontës, The. *Selected Poems*
*Browning, Robert. *Men and Women and other poems*
*Burns, Robert. *The Kilmarnock Poems*
*Chaucer, Geoffrey, *Canterbury Tales*
*Clare, John. *Selected Poems*
*Coleridge, Samuel Taylor. *Poems*
*Donne, John. *The Complete English Poems*
**Elizabethan Sonnets*
**English Moral Interludes*
**Everyman and Medieval Miracle Plays*
**Everyman's Book of Evergreen Verse*
**Everyman's Book of Victorian Verse*
*Gay, John. *The Beggar's Opera and other eighteenth-century plays*
**The Golden Treasury of Longer Poems*
*Hardy, Thomas. *Selected Poems*
*Herbert, George. *The English Poems*
*Hopkins, Gerard Manley. *The Major Poems*
Ibsen, Henrik
**A Doll's House; The Wild Duck; The Lady from the Sea*
**Hedda Gabler; The Master Builder; John Gabriel Borkman*

*Keats, John. *Poems*
*Langland, William. *The Vision of Piers Plowman*
*Marlowe, Christopher. *Complete Plays and Poems*
*Marvell, Andrew. *Complete Poetry*
*Middleton, Thomas. *Three Plays*
*Milton, John. *Complete Poems*
**Palgrave's Golden Treasury*
**Pearl, Cleanness, Patience* and *Sir Gawain and the Green Knight*
**Poems of the Second World War*
*Pope, Alexander. *Collected Poems*
**Restoration Plays*
**The Rubáiyát of Omar Khayyám and other Persian poems*
*Shelley, Percy Bysshe. *Selected Poems*
**Six Middle English Romances*
*Spenser, Edmund. *The Faerie Queene: Books I to III*
**The Stuffed Owl*
*Synge, J.M. *Plays, Poems and Prose*
*Tennyson, Alfred. *In Memoriam, Maud and other poems*
Thomas, Dylan
  **Collected Poems, 1934–1952*
  **The Poems*
  **Under Milk Wood*
*Webster and Ford. *Selected Plays*
*Wilde, Oscar. *Plays, Prose Writings and Poems*
*Wordsworth, William. *Selected Poems*

RELIGION AND PHILOSOPHY

*Bacon, Francis. *The Advancement of Learning*
*Berkeley, George. *Philosophical Works*
**The Buddha's Philosophy of Man*
*Carlyle, Thomas. *Sartor Resartus*
**Chinese Philosophy in Classical Times*
*Descartes, René. *A Discourse on Method*
**Hindu Scriptures*
*Hobbes, Thomas. *Leviathan*
*Kant, Immanuel. *A Critique of Pure Reason*
**The Koran*
*Leibniz, Gottfried Wilhelm. *Philosophical Writings*

*Locke, John. *An Essay Concerning Human Understanding (abridgement)*
*More, Thomas. *Utopia*
Pascal, Blaise. *Pensées*
Plato. *The Trial and Death of Socrates*
**The Ramayana and Mahábhárata*
*Spinoza, Benedictus de. *Ethics*

SCIENCES: POLITICAL AND GENERAL

Coleridge, Samuel Taylor. *On the Constitution of the Church and State*
Derry, John. *English Politics and the American Revolution*
Harvey, William. *The Circulation of the Blood and other writings*
*Locke, John. *Two Treatises of Government*
*Machiavelli, Niccolò. *The Prince and other political writings*
*Malthus, Thomas. *An Essay on the Principle of Population*
*Mill, J.S. *Utilitarianism; On Liberty: Representative Government*
*Plato. *The Republic*
*Ricardo, David. *Principles of Political Economy and Taxation*
Rousseau, J.-J.
  **Emile*
  **The Social Contract* and *Discourses*
*Wollstonecraft, Mary. *A Vindication of the Rights of Woman*

TRAVEL AND TOPOGRAPHY

Boswell, James. *The Journal of a Tour to the Hebrides*
Darwin, Charles. *The Voyage of the 'Beagle'*
*Hudson, W.H. *Idle Days in Patagonia*
*Kingsley, Mary. *Travels in West Africa*
*Stevenson, R.L. *An Inland Voyage; Travels with a Donkey; The Silverado Squatters*
*Thomas, Edward. *The South Country*
**Travels of Marco Polo*
*White, Gilbert. *The Natural History of Selborne*